Jenny Yates Hammett

Woman's Transformations: A Psychological Theology

**Symposium Series
Volume Eight**

THE EDWIN MELLEN PRESS
New York and Toronto

Copyright © 1982, The Edwin Mellen Press

Symposium Series: ISBN 0-88946-989-X
Volume Eight: ISBN 0-88946-918-0

Cover quilt designed and pieced by Nancy Crow. Hand-quilting by
Mrs. Levi Mast. Titled: *November I*, © 1980, Baltimore, Ohio, 64" x
64".
Photograph courtesy of the artist.

Back cover photograph: Laurie Roberts
Diagrams: Diane Krueger

For information:

The Edwin Mellen Press
P.O. Box 450
Lewiston, New York 14092

Library of Congress Cataloging in Publication Data

Hammett, Jenny Yates.
   Woman's Transformations.

   (Symposium series; v. 8)
   1. Woman (Christian theology) 2. Women—Psychology.
I. Title. II. Series: Symposium series
(Edwin Mellen Press); v. 8
BT704.H35 1982   230 .088042   82-14287
ISBN 0-88946-918-0

Printed in the United States of America.

To a Guide of Great Wisdom
Stanley Romaine Hopper

Contents

Acknowledgements

First, my appreciation and dedication of the work to my mentor, Stanley Hopper, who taught me that the turn comes in trusting the tracks and this left me prepared to become my own guide. Also I wish to acknowledge the deep influence of David Miller, who opened my vision to the multifacets of the other sides of the quest.

My thanks to Ann Ulanov, who left a map of the bridge between Jungian psychology and Christian theology. And my gratitude to the women of Colgate/Rochester/Bexley Hall seminary whose quest for priesthood in the Episcopal church led me to write the original lectures which comprise the first part of the text in response to their questioning whether the God of the Judaic-Christian tradition was only male.

The first chapter is a revision of an article originally published in *Religion in Life*. I am grateful for their policy of allowing the author to retain copyright following first publication.

I wish to thank two former Wells College students who became teachers for me: Amy Kindrick taught me to read the stories of religion as patterns through which we suffer, and Joanne Scandale, a poet, helped me find the bridge between the image and its embodiment in language.

Maria Hyland gave the words readable form through her typing. Herbert Richardson wrote and asked about my manuscript at a time that I was putting "notes on a vision" away in a desk drawer to begin another book.

Finally, my special thanks to Hugh who lived through this phase of the quest with me.

God "as"

"Metaphor bridges the abyss between God and self. Hence, it is in this 'between' that one learns to talk of God 'as'."

1

God "as"

When I first heard women raising the question why God couldn't be a "she," it struck me as a misplaced concern and as bad theology. I wondered why the women didn't spend their time on something more useful, such as addressing problems of discrimination in concrete situations.

I encountered the issue again as a professor at Colgate Rochester/Bexley Hall/Crozer Seminary. Many of the women students, in the face of the problems of ordination in the Episcopal Church, were asking one question: not, What can we do about the authority structures of the church that exclude women? but rather, Is the God of the Judaic-Christian tradition only male?

Although I still thought the issue misplaced, I began to see the connection between the concrete situation and the problem of naming God. Those who respond to the problem simply by changing God's name and sex or color seem to have missed the point of contemporary theology's contribution to the problem of talking about God.

Hence, I would like to put the God-talk of liberation theology into perspective. After attempting to

3

unravel the many strands of contemporary thought on religion, I have decided to follow through on two that I find most useful for seeing the place of liberation theory. First, I would like to present Sigmund Freud's theory of the origin of the father God concept and, second, Paul Tillich's notion of the God beyond the God of theism.

Liberation theology is the name commonly used for the theologies that have arisen out of the experience of oppression of particular groups such as blacks, women, Indians, and Third World countries. To illustrate that each group moves from the situation of oppression to naming God in its own particular image, you have only to listen to some of the language: God is Red, God is Black, God is Androgynous Being, God fights on the side of the oppressed. Each attempts to combat the projected authority image of God as white father that has been used to sanction those created in his image and to exclude others.

It is in the function of breaking the idol of a literalized father God that liberation theology joins Freud and Tillich. The problem, however, is that many liberation theologians have not learned from history and consequently run the risk of repeating the literalism and the exclusiveness.

For example, James Cone, the major spokesman for black liberation theology, writes: "The blackness of God, and everything implied by it in a racist society, is the heart of Black Theology's doctrine of God. There is no place in Black Theology for a colorless God in a society when people suffer precisely because of their color. The black theologian must reject any conception of God which stifles black self-determination by picturing God as a God of all peoples."[1]

Whereas James Cone's criterion for God language is color, Mary Daly's is sex. In her book *Beyond God the Father*, she wrote:

> It is becoming clear that if God-language is even
> implicitly compatible with oppressiveness, . . .
> then it will either have to be developed in such a
> way that it becomes explicitly relevant to the
> problem of sexism or else dismissed . . . . In my
> thinking, the specific criterion which implies a
> mandate to reject certain forms of God-talk is ex-
> pressed in the question: . . . . Does it *encourage*
> human becoming toward psychological and so-
> cial fulfillment, toward an androgynous mode of
> living?[2]

According to Bishop J.A.T. Robinson, when an image becomes a substitute for God "so that what is not
embodied in the image is excluded or denied, then we
have a new idolatry,"[3] and the iconoclastic task begins
again.

The idolatry in some liberation theology is relative-
ly easy to criticize. But apparently the role of the father
God of theism is not so obvious. To trace the function
of the image in contemporary theology, let us begin first
with a summary of Freud's discussion of the origin of
the God concept. The sources include *The Future of an
Illusion, Totem and Taboo, Moses and Monotheism*,
and *Leonardo Da Vinci*. Psychoanalysis, Freud wrote,

> has taught us the intimate connection between
> the father complex and belief in God, has shown
> us that the personal God is psychologically noth-
> ing but an exalted father, and demonstrates to
> us how youthful persons lose their religious belief
> as soon as the authority of the father breaks
> down . . . . Religiousness is biologically traced to
> the long period of helplessness and need of help
> of the little child. When the child grows up and
> realizes his loneliness and weakness in the pres-
> ence of the great forces of life, he then perceives
> his condition as in childhood and seeks to disarm

> his despair through a regressive revival of the
> protecting forces of childhood.[4]

The child paints an all-powerful, all-knowing, all-good, ever-present face over the threatening forces. These attributes, Freud documents clinically, bring to view the father figure behind the divine image. With God painted as a single person, the "relation to him could recover the intimacy and intensity of the child's relation to his father." Once the image of God the father is established, then people move to viewing themselves as God's chosen people—the favorite son idea. Freud notes especially that this phase of development of religious ideas is followed by the concept of the "white Christian civilization," citing in particular "pious America's claim to being God's own country."[5]

As an aside, it is noteworthy that this is precisely the current role ascribed to God in the liberation theologies of some developing Third World countries.

Religious ideas—and the God concept in particular—arise, Freud contended, from the wish to put a protecting face on the threatening forces of nature and the desire "to rectify the short-comings of civilization which have made themselves painfully felt."[6] God the father is an illusion according to Freud. And by illusion he simply means that which is derived from human wishes. Illusions need not necessarily be false. That is, there may or may not be a basis in reality for the wish. Many have misunderstood Freud, thinking he was making an empirical claim, namely that religion or God is a delusion or erroneous belief. Rather, Freud could only say how an image functioned in the psyche of his patients and how the subsequent religious ideas functioned in civilization.

It is within this context that I think Freud's analysis can be useful in understanding on a deeper level the current God imagery in liberation theology. At issue is whether religious ideas that arise out of a desire to put a familiar, protecting face on threatening forces and out of a desire to rectify the shortcomings of civilization necessarily give rise to God as a father figure. I think not. Rather it seems that the father symbol is only one of an entire constellation of symbols that refer to one's mythical origins. I do not wish to get too far sidetracked into Freudian criticism, but it is well known that Freud assigned to the myth of the primal murder of the father an unwarranted historical or empirical basis. Religious symbols arise out of one's mythic origins and have the potential to point toward the sacred. Freud never demythologized his own fantasies of the primal killing of the father; it was, he believed, an actual event.

Why is it that although the mother is the first object of protection, one projects the father's face as protector? Freud was never able to explain the rise of female deities in his theory of religious illusions.

How could we detect an authentic change in religious symbolism? In order to evaluate the new symbols in liberation theology, I would like to turn now to Paul Tillich's theory of religious symbols.

Symbols, Tillich contended, arise out of a group's acknowledging that in this word or thing its own being participates. A symbol is not invented intentionally but arises out of a change in the group's unconscious level of identification. If someone tries to invent a symbol, it becomes accepted only when the unconscious of a group says yes to it. Likewise, symbols die when they no longer express a reality in which the group participates. The symbol ceases to communicate in failing to open a dimension of reality. A symbol arises out of the dimension of depth in the self and functions to communicate the depth dimension of reality.

To use Tillich's criteria to evaluate the symbolism of liberation theology, one first asks whether the situation out of which the father symbol arose has changed and, if so, whether the symbol still functions to communicate a reality in which those who use the symbol participate. Furthermore, one asks whether the new symbolism is arising out of the emerging consciousness in new situations or whether the symbols are artificially invented. First, let us discuss the question of the current state of the situation out of which the symbol of the father God arose.

Partly because of Freud's influence, there is a clear trend in contemporary Protestant theology away from the father God of traditional theism. Tillich speaks of transcending theism toward a God beyond God. God as a being over against the self too easily becomes an object for idolatry. Instead, Tillich proposes to view God as the ground of all being. Anything is potentially a symbol for pointing to this depth dimension of reality.

In response to Freud's theory of God as a projection of the father image, Tillich replied that "every projection is not only a projection *of* something, but it is also a projection *upon* something. What is this 'something' upon which the image of the father is 'projected' so that it becomes divine? The answer can only be: It is projected upon the 'screen' of the unconditional! And this screen is not projected. It makes projection possible.[7] Although this screen of the unconditional points to the influence of idealism on Tillich's view, his point has relevance for our problem of evaluating the God symbolism. To identify the concrete media or symbol of the unconditional with the unconditional itself is, he says, religiously speaking "idolatry" and psychologically speaking "neurotic."

According to Tillich, the father God of theism, which has become an object over against the self as object, must die before the God beyond God can be known and before one has the courage to be as an authentic self. Tillich's analysis is very close to Freud's analysis of the primal father who must be killed to free the individual for self-development.

Keep in mind that I am simply trying to document the situation that precedes the influx of new symbolism in the theology of the 1970's. Freud wrote *The Future of an Illusion* in 1927 and Tillich *The Courage to Be* in 1952. By the 1960's their ideas had become popularized. In 1963 Bishop John Robinson, in his widely read work *Honest to God*, reflected the views not only of Tillich's God beyond theism but also the influence of Rudolf Bultmann's demythologizing and Dietrich Bonhoeffer's religionless Christianity. Also acknowledging his debt to Nietzche, Robinson wrote that the image of the supreme father in heaven must die if the individual is to be free.

The question remains whether the situation that gave rise to the father image is changing. Clearly it is changing in the minds of theologians, but what about the larger situation? Robinson addressed the issue:

> Few Christians have been able to understand the vehemence of the revolt because for them he has not been the tyrant they portrayed, who impoverishes, enslaves and annihilates man. Indeed, for most non-Christians also he has been more of a Grandfather in heaven, a kindly Old Man who could be pushed into one corner while they got on with the business of life . . . . Can he be rehabilitated, or is it the whole conception of that sort of a God, "up there," "out there," or however one likes to put it, a projection, an idol, that can and should be torn down?[8]

Once a symbol dies there are two possible paths for theology to follow. If the symbol or image has been assumed to be identical with the reality, then when the symbol dies the reality itself is said to be dead. The other path is to acknowledge the necessity of images to talk about God and wait for new ones to emerge out of a changing situation or invent false ones.

The theologies of the 1960's and 1970's have followed both paths.

As Robinson foresaw, if the image was identified with the reality, when the father image out there is no longer operative then God himself will die.

Three years following the bishop's warning, the cover of *Time* claimed "God Is Dead." The claim was not that the image of God is dead, but rather God is dead. Thomas Altizer hoped aloud that theology could transcend the language of images. Without images Altizer's only alternative was to claim God's death as a historical event. The reason he felt compelled to make this seemingly absurd claim was that the father God of theism was no longer a meaningful reality in the lives of most people.

The other path, the one advocated by Robinson and Tillich, is to acknowledge the necessity of symbols in order to talk about God. Unlike Tillich, Robinson writes that "it may be impossible to imagine the personal ground of our being except as an almighty Individual, endowed with a center of consciousness and will like ourselves."[9] The problem is not the images per se. Rather the problem is the identification of a particular image with God to the exclusion of all other perception and imaginings. To demythologize—in this view—is not to assume we can talk about God without myth and symbol but rather to see the relativity of the forms of our imaginings.

And in precisely this context and out of this history, I think we can begin to understand and criticize the rise of multiple images of God in recent liberation theology. Let us now turn briefly to some representative examples.

Mary Daly, one of the leading theologians in women's liberation theology, wrote:

The biblical and popular image of God as a great patriarch in heaven, rewarding and punishing according to his mysterious and seemingly arbitrary will, has dominated the imagination of millions over thousands of years. The symbol of the Father God, spawned in the human imagination and sustained as plausible by patriarchy, has in turn rendered service to this type of society by making its mechanisms for the oppression of women appear right and fitting . . . . The images and values of a given society have been projected into the realm of dogmas and "Articles of Faith," and these in turn justify the social structures which have given rise to them and which sustain their plausibility.[10]

The problem, she contends, is that women have had the power of naming stolen from them. To exist humanely is to name oneself, the world, and God. Daly's method of liberation is through the naming of oneself as woman and to use woman as a name for God.[11] The theological base is the affirmation that woman is created in the image of God.

To understand her theory on naming, I find Paul Ricoeur's analysis of Freud's preference for the father symbol useful. He asks why the father figure has a privilege for conveying God that the mother figure lacks. He concludes that it is because of the father's function as name-giver and law-giver. And also, "because he is the name-giver, he is the name-problem, as the Hebrews first conceived him."[12]

Mary Daly asks for the power of naming as the meaning of liberation; James Cone, spokesman for black theology, says that liberation means that the oppressed must define reality, self and God included, for themselves, "without taking their cues from the oppressors."[13]

Recall that Freud, in tracing the origin of the father God concept, said that once the image or name of God is established, then the people move to viewing themselves as God's chosen people. He pointed out that this was the path followed by white Christian civilization. Now listen to a spokesman for black Christian civilization. Cone writes, "The blackness of God means that God has made the oppressed condition his own condition . . . . His election of Israel . . . reveals that the *liberation* of the oppressed is a part of the innermost nature of God himself."[14]

The next step, Freud said, is that God is viewed as fighting for my side. Recall his illustration of America's claiming to be God's country. James Cone writes: "Because God has made the goal of black people his own goal, Black Theology believes that it is not only appropriate but necessary to begin the doctrine of God with an insistence on his blackness . . . . Knowing God means being on the side of the oppressed."[15]

Thus far I hope to have shown two things: first, that the concepts "God is Black" and "God is Female" have arisen in much the same manner in which Freud said the concept "God is Father" arose. Furthermore, I think these new symbols can be understood out of the context of the rush to fill the void of a dying symbolism. The political and social situation of the 1960's obviously gave rise to the awakening self-assertion of the various oppressed groups. But why each group proceeds to name God in its own image is not so immediately clear. The second thing I hope to have shown is that liberation theologians could benefit from the twentieth-century criticism of the literalizing of the father God concept. Quite obviously the new images that exclude all other perceptions and imaginings run the risk of a new idolatry.

All theologies, whether done from the viewpoint of a white male, a black, or a female, will be abortive of the liberation sought unless they rise to a perspective that is not exclusive.

In an attempt to retain the particularism but to avoid the exclusiveness, I have a very simple proposal to make in terms of the structure of our talk about God. Rather than claiming God *is* Black or God *is* Father, I suggest we make clear our symbolic intent and speak of God *as* Father or God *as* Mother. Through the *as* structure we could open a possibility for a rebirth of symbols without necessarily remaking the idols.

Stanley Hopper cues us to the philosophical structure of "something as something," spelled out by Martin Heidegger in *Being and Time*.[16] One speaks of a particular phenomenon *as* bringing to appearance an aspect of the larger structure of being. Such a structure takes the particular into account but does not exclude other possible manifestations of being.

Perhaps this phenomenological approach when used to talk about the nature of the self in relation to the nature of God could avoid some of the problems inherent in an empirical or idealist approach.

Also the structure of "God *as*" could open new avenues for addressing the polynonymous God and anonymous God who says only, "I am."[17]

Indeed, this crucial issue was addressed in Hebrew scripture where God and Moses converse together on the hills of Midian. There the bargain was struck whereby God called Moses to lead the liberation from Egypt, the Exodus that became the central event by which Israel was to interpret her history. Yet, when Moses received his commission, he did not ask any of the questions one would expect a freedom fighter to raise: Where will I get the armies to defeat Pharaoh? How will we get to the place we are going? The verses of Exodus 3 describe the strange conversation: "But if they ask me what his name is, that is, the name of the liberator, what am I to tell them?" And God said to

Moses, "I am who I am . . . . This is my name for all time; by this name I shall be invoked for all generations to come."

We have the image of a God who picks and cares for a particular people but who also refuses to give them a name whereby the God can be limited. And we come full circle again to the problem of contemporary theology.

How can we talk about this kind of God? It seems to me, at least, that the language structure "God as" is one way we could allow what Kenneth Burke has called the right of everyone to worship God in his or her own metaphor.

Metaphor consists in giving something a name that belongs to something else, a transference across or between. It is this dimension between self and God that gives rise to the possibility of doing theology symbolically.

Metaphor bridges the abyss between God and self. Hence it is in this "between" that one learns to talk of God 'as.' Metaphor arises out of the juxtaposition of a dimension of one thing with a hitherto unrevealed dimension of an apparently totally dissimilar thing.

The dimension of God in the Judaic-Christian tradition hitherto unrevealed is the feminine. Perhaps it can only come into vision as women deepen their consciousness of themselves.

Hence my project is to look at the stages in Judaic-Christian religious consciousness as a move across from the emerging human consciousness. Specifically, I am moving toward the place of the feminine consciousness as it gives rise to religious vision and naming.

Notes

1. Cone, *A Black Theology of Liberation* (Philadelphia, Lippincott, 1970), p. 120.
2. Daly, *Beyond God the Father* (Boston: Beacon Press, 1973), p. 21.
3. Robinson, *Honest to God* (Philadelphia: Westminster Press, 1963), p. 125.
4. Freud, *Leonardo Da Vinci: A Study in Psychosexuality* (New York: Random House, 1916), p. 98.
5. Freud, *The Future of an Illusion* (Garden City, N.Y.: Doubleday, 1961), pp. 27-28.
6. *Ibid.*, p. 30.
7. Tillich, *Theology of Culture* (New York: Oxford University Press, 1959), p. 140.
8. *Honest to God*, p. 41.
9. *Ibid.*, pp. 131-32.
10. *Beyond God the Father*, p. 13.
11. *Ibid.*, p. 8.
12. Ricoeur, *Freud and Philosophy* (New Haven: Yale University Press, 1970), p. 542.
13. *A Black Theology of Liberation*, p. 118.
14. *Ibid.*, p. 121.
15. *Ibid.*, pp. 121, 124.
16. Heidegger, *Being and Time* (New York: Harper & Row, 1962), pp. 188-93. See Hopper and Miller, eds., *Interpretation: The Poetry of Meaning* (New York: Harcourt Brace, 1967), p. xvi.
17. I use the word "polynonymous" advisedly to avoid the possibility of multiple literalisms of theism in the current term "polytheism."

Creation and the Female-Male Image

"If to be created in the image of God is to be created female and male, then one way to do a logos of God is by understanding what it is to be male and female."

2

Creation and the Female-Male Image

Today, women seeking to break out of traditional roles are often told "Don't do anything that is not feminine!" But what is it to be feminine? Is there such a thing as feminine nature, whether fixed or in the process of becoming? Perhaps we need to ask why theology offers so little aid. Have theologians indeed been referring to the generic when they wrote the nature and destiny of man?

First, let us examine what theologians have said when they addressed the issue of what it is to be created female. Some representative traditional theologians should help us understand the need for reformulation of the nature of the feminine.

Augustine says that the male alone is created in the image of God. Woman is created in the image of man, not the image of God. Hence at best she is a second hand image of God and always subordinate to the male. Augustine in *The Trinity* writes:

> According to the argument I have already developed in my discussion of the human mind, it fol-

lows that a woman can be said to be "an image of God" when we consider her together with her husband. This is because, when a man and a woman are considered together, the idea of "image of God" applies to both. However, if we consider a woman alone, in her status as a "helpmeet" (a word which refers to woman alone), then she is not "an image of God." But a man alone is an image of God even though a woman alone is not. In fact, a man alone is as fully an image of God as he is when considered together with a woman.

Clement of Alexanderia in the *Stromata* admonishes woman to blush with shame when she considers of what nature she is.

The Aristotelian idea of fixed natures was picked up by Thomas Aquinas in terms of the nature of the feminine and passed through the ages through the dogma of the Catholic church. The nature of the feminine is to be subordinate to the male, subordination being part of the status of a biologically inferior being. One way to overcome the inferior nature was by way of virginity, leading to an idealization of the Virgin Mother.

Because the feminine has in large part in the history of theology been either omitted from creation in God's image or simply given an inferior status, I would like to start over again to develop a basis for correlation of theology—the logos of God—with images of the feminine.

The basis of such a theology is Genesis 1:26-27:

> Then God said, Let us make mankind in our image after our likeness . . . So God created mankind in his own image, in the image of God he created him; male and female he created them.

The word for God is 'Elohim,' the plural form containing both male and female roots. Biblical scholars are always at a loss to explain the plural reference 'in our image,' usually suggesting such things as other heavenly beings. Theologians through the ages have speculated about what it is to be created in the image of God. But I see no way around "in our image" being modified by the clause "male and female created he them."

If to be created in the image of God is to be created female and male, then one way to do a logos of God is by understanding what it is to be male and female. And perhaps then we might move beyond a God who is known for omnipotence.

Twentieth century theology has usually been divided between the followers of Karl Barth and Paul Tillich. Barth did exegete the creation narrative in terms of the male-female referring to God's image but hastened to add woman's subordination to the man being like man's subordination to God. Barth never demythologized the Biblical patriarchal world view in his understanding of woman. Tillich on the other hand begins with experience and develops a theology of polarities which encompasses the potentialities traditionally divided between male and female. Wholeness of being requires holding the potentialities in juxtaposition in all beings.

I too am suggesting a theology which starts more explicitly with what it is to be created in the female-male polarity. Images of what it is to be created female should open new understanding of what it is to be created in the image of God.

I shall seek to open new images of the feminine for theology by way of correlation with the work of Carl Jung. Let us start with the female-male polarity. Jung develops the psychological feminine as it appears in both male and female. Each sex contains the psychological potential of the opposite sex. The presence of the feminine in the male is the anima, and the presence of the masculine in the female is the animus.

Polarity refers to both male and female present and interacting toward wholeness of selfhood. Polarity turns to polarization from fearing and suppressing that which one considers alien to one's identity. Polarization currently manifests itself in terms of the dominance of one-sided male consciousness. Modern Apollonian consciousness is at a dead end for lack of the wisdom of Sophia. Our patriarchal images have become graven images, and we seek releasement from the idolatry of our ways of apprehending the world.

We must return to the feminine side of the polarity to open new images. Jung aids us by way of the feminine archetypes, constellations of the recurring images of the feminine in the history of consciousness. All too often feminists have overlooked this repository because the archetypal feminine in our day has been reduced to the virgin mother ideal. As a starting point for study, let us look at a grouping of the images in terms of developmental stages of the feminine following the formulation of one of Jung's disciples, Eric Neumann.

The first stage is the image of mother. The positive value of this image is the woman's finding the feminine self through identification with the mother. The danger lies in fixation at this stage, never developing one's own self identity apart from mother, mothering, or mother role models. I often reflect on the current desire for role models as a source of feminine identity formation in light of the mother fixation—in spite of the popular renunciation of "mothering."

The negative manifestation of mothering lies in the self sacrificing aspect of the maternal woman. Thus far the feminist movement has focused on the need for the woman to consider her own needs but not on her suffocating effects on others. Because the mother may renounce herself in the process of concern for the other, she may become overprotective and possessive of what she considers her due in returned affections. Hence she all too often hinders the growth of those for whom she has sacrificed her life—at least those unlived portions. She projects this unlived ''masculine'' possibility onto son or even daughter and forever expects someone else to actualize her ideal.

In the second stage of development of the feminine, the daughter attempts to live out her father's image of the ideal female, his anima. This second dependency stage is that of espousal of patriarchal values and, like the first, runs the risk of fixation, especially in our culture with its patriarchal base. Society all too often fosters this arrested development where women are forever the daughter of a father as basic identity. Women living in this stage expect other women also to depend on father figures as a basic dependent way of life.

The role model for women at this stage is simply to try to live out those images projected upon her, again never forming independent selfhood. To move beyond this stage the woman must develop her own animus. The female ego must begin to call its own those potentialities formerly feared as other than the self, the overpowering masculine.

In the third stage of development the masculine side of woman assumes outward form as the hero who rescues her from the father and forms a partnership. This hero is again potentially a woman's own animus, but she usually projects rather than integrates. If it is projected in marriage one ends with a patriarchal marriage; again the woman forever looks for her potentiality to emerge in her husband. Failure to reintegrate one's possibilities may lead to continuous projections, as in extramarital affairs.

Esther Harding calls these projections, forever desired and forever unattained, the "ghostly lover." The love may be directed toward any figure who embodies one's ideal: politician, professor, minister, or therapist. The polarity of female-male is attained only in fantasy.

The problem may be overcome in the fourth stage when the woman discovers the opposite sex potentially within her own selfhood. One's children, father, mother, or husband no longer define one's identity. And at this stage when the woman integrates the masculine she then returns to integrate the feminine.

The present women's movement is still in the process of fighting for a chance to develop those potentialities heretofore reserved for the male. It is hardly surprising that there is a split with those women happy in their mothering roles. Only in the fourth stage can this dichotomy be overcome.

Western theology has yet to develop a concept of the polarity of female-male as the basis of wholeness such as the yin-yang.

We are seeking a new creation, a theology of the human in which, as Paul envisions in Galatians 3:28, "There is neither Jew nor Greek, there is neither slave nor free, there is neither male nor female for you are all one in Christ Jesus."

Sin and the Image
of the Feminine

". . . woman for too long has been the scapegoat
in the doctrine of sin."

3

Sin and the Image
of the Feminine

There are three basic areas which I would like us to consider about sin and the feminine.

First, let us look at the image of the feminine as set forth by the representative "Fathers" of the church in their doctrines of sin.

Second, I shall briefly re-examine the myth of the fall in terms of four basic functions of mythology—the metaphysical, the cosmological, the sociological, and the psychological.

And third, I shall attempt a revision—that is, give a new picture—of the psychological dimension of the myth of the fall through the female-male imagery in the developmental psychology of Carl Jung.

In our consideration of the creation we followed the Priestly account in Genesis 1. We move now to the Yahwistic account of creation and fall in Genesis 2 and 3.

First, let us look at some of the traditional theological images of woman in the doctrine of the fall, having their origin in Genesis 2 and 3. One of the most misogynous comes from Tertullian.

In pains and anxieties dost thou bear children, woman; and toward thine husband is thy inclination, and he lords it over thee. And do you not know that you are each an Eve? The sentence of God on this sex of yours lives in this age: the guilt must of necessity live too. You are the devil's gateway; you are the unsealer of that forbidden tree; you are the first deserter of the divine law: you are she who persuaded him whom the devil was not valiant enough to attack. You destroyed so easily God's image, man. On account of your desert—that is, death—the Son of God had to die.

Irenaeus in *Adversus Haereses* tried to absolve Adam of any blame by attributing all sin to Eve and the serpent.

The seduction of Eve by the snake led Augustine to viewing woman's bodily nature as the source of all corruption. And then through the corrupt body of woman original sin is passed through every act of generation.

The illustrations are endless but these should suffice to let you see that woman for too long has been the scapegoat in the doctrine of sin.

We must review the myth which shapes our place in the world and our psychological journey from birth to death. In order to look again at the myth of the fall, I would like to use the universal functions of mythology as developed by Joseph Campbell in his four volume work, *The Masks of God*.

The first function is one of reconciliation of awakening consciousness with the mystery of its beginnings. The development of self-consciousness always presupposes a return to one's origins. For example, the patient in psychotherapy gains insight by returning to those mysterious beginnings of life. As we know well from Freud, the beginnings transcend the empirical event, reaching the archetypal level of myth.

It is important in the development of feminine consciousness that we go beyond the empirical events of
daily life to the mythology of the creation of female and
male. And here we would seek to understand male and
female as the image of God.

The second function of mythology is to render a
cosmology, an image of the universe. Biblical scholars,
except for the literalists, have long agreed on the need
to demythologize the six day creation story in light of
current scientific theories. And of course there is
another brand of literalists, the scientific positivists,
who still try to reconcile the two different levels of
discourse: myth and science. But for all useful purposes
the science and creation battle is over.

Although Biblical scholars have readily demythologized the outdated cosmology, they have yet
to see the need to demythologize the sociological
world view in the myth of the fall. The third function of
mythology, the sociological, serves to validate and
maintain a specific social order. The myth of the fall was
used from Biblical times to the present day to validate
and give authority to a patriarchal society. In a patriarchal society the image of woman is as a secondary, inferior, and dependent being whose worth is constituted
in producing the male genealogy. The myth of the fall
validates the existing social order of patriarchal
Judaism; the fact that man ruled over women in the
society was given religious sanction by calling man's
rule over woman a "curse" for tempting Adam.

Woman's place as a secondary being is well
established in the Old Testament world through law.
Note for example the two following passages from
Leviticus 12 and 27: "If a woman conceives and bears a
male child, then she shall be unclean seven days . . .
But if she bears a female child, then she shall be
unclean two weeks." In cultic practice the "valuation
of a male from twenty years old to sixty years old shall

be fifty shekels of silver . . . If the person is a female, your valuation shall be thirty shekels."

Looking back from the Exodus, the Hebrew people formulate a myth that validates the patriarchal order of their society with woman as slave, concubine, harlot, wife, daughter, and mother. Only a few manage to rise above the system as merchants and prophets.

Just as was the case in the Old Testament world, so today the myth of the fall is still used to prove the sacredness of a passing social and ecclesiastical order. Recently, for example, I heard a television debate in which a man argued against passage of the Equal Rights Amendment for women on the grounds that such equality was contrary to our religious heritage. That women are still regarded as secondary and inferior beings by elements of organized religion was evidenced in the recent problem in the Episcopal church over the ordination of women.

Although religious doctrines are often watered down in the church so as to appear innocuous, at the mythical level the fall is still a powerful determinant in our society and our psyches. The question is, what is to be done? Should the doctrine be discarded or does it yet have something to say? I strongly believe that theologians must seek to make the doctrines such as the fall understandable for our present age, in order to correct the injustice to half the human race.

I find the best way to understand the function of mythology is to see how it fosters the psychological centering and unfolding development of the individual. In trying to see in what sense the myth of the fall is a psychology of our present existence, the sense in which we are all Eve and Adam, I shall attempt to see the dynamics of the fall in light of Carl Jung's developmental stages.

In the first stage of development the child, whether female or male, identifies with the mother, experiencing the security of undifferentiated wholeness. In the adult the stage may persist as dreaming innocence or non-actualized potentiality. One can easily see the correlation with the pre-fall state of innocence.

In the second stage both male and female differentiate themselves from mother through the encounter with the opposite sex as father. The male begins to identify with his father, and the female becomes dependent upon the father. The awareness of opposites at this stage marks the alienation from an innocent pre-sexual wholeness.

Again one can easily see the correlate state in the fall. Eve desires to actualize her potentiality, to know good and evil, to differentiate the opposites, a step in all emerging self-consciousness. In the fall, as in the second stage of development, there is an awareness of the sexual opposites male and female. Genesis 3:7 says the eyes of both were opened, and they knew they were naked.

The state of being caught between the desire to actualize one's freedom and the desire to preserve the dreaming innocence of undifferentiated wholeness is anxiety. Temptation is the state between possibility and actualization of potentiality. This state just prior to the leap or the fall is anxiety.

One is anxious over unlimited freedom: "You shall become like the gods, knowing good and evil." There is a very thin line between natural self-affirmation as creature in the image of God, which is necessary for all development, and the destructive self-elevation to the place of God.

In fact, it is the image of God in the self which makes the fall a possibility. The failure to affirm oneself as created in God's image or to actualize one's potentialities is sloth. I suspect that sloth is a greater problem today than is hubris or the self-elevation to the place of God.

Harvey Cox says that Eve shares with Adam the dominion over the earth and all its creatures. Yet she gives up her responsibility and self-determination in letting the snake tell her what to do.

Jung, in tracing snake imagery in psychology and literature, locates woman's encounter with the snake in the second stage of development, where she is over-powered by the masculine. Like the mother archetype of the first stage, the father archetype has both a good, or divine, side and a terrible, or evil, side. Woman caught between the commands of both "God" and the "Devil" in the Genesis account fails to develop her own identity. Woman caught between good and evil is the image of woman in patriarchal consciousness.

Soren Kierkegaard says sin is the despairing refusal to be one's self. To become what she was created to be, a woman, in the image of God, must choose her own identity and not allow herself to be named by the expectations of the prevailing consciousness. To become resolute is to choose one's possibilities for being, in spite of public opinion. To be irresolute is to let the snake tell you what to do.

The tension between freedom and destiny must always be acknowledged in any discussion of sin and potentiality. The self is free insofar as it can deliberate and choose beyond conditioning. In the myth of the fall, desires and external forces do influence Eve's and Adam's decisions to eat the fruit. Yet for the concept of decision to make sense, it must in some sense be free. Human beings, because of their reciprocal social influence on each other, experience sin as a "condition." However, since each individual chooses and adds to the sin of the race, it is sin as choice and act which limits human freedom and destiny.

Eve's choice, although conditioned by what she is told to do or not to do within the Father archetype, is still her choice to attain consciousness of the opposites, whether good or evil, male or female.

In the move between stages of development, a higher level of consciousness is like a burden of guilt. The sacredness of a prior stage has been challenged. These are no problems without consciousness, but would we have every woman and every man remain in innocence and non-development?

The third stage of development is the stage of heroes. The male moves from his father identification to his own manhood, and the female may either project her so-called masculine potentialities onto a male hero or develop them within herself.

I would like to suggest Eve as the model of the female asserting those potentialities hitherto limited to the male. Eve is tempted to develop her knowledge of good and evil, to defy the command of the good Father. She storms the heavens and turns the world upside down, calling forth the wrath of patriarchal judgement. Since Adam is simply the passive recipient of the fruit, Eve must be cursed to be ruled over by Adam in order to reverse the passive role of Adam and the aggressive, self-assertive role of Eve in the first sin.

In many ways women, in the present task of liberating their potentialities, identify with Eve. Like Eve, women are storming such sacred sanctuaries as the tables down at Mory's and the alters of the Episcopal church, defying those bounds imposed upon them.

Christian Salvation
and
Feminine Transformation

". . . in the history of all consciousness the hero myth leads into the myth of self transformation, the myth of divine daughter or son. We are moving back to reclaiming self in the image of God."

4

Christian Salvation
and Feminine Transformation

The hero stage is one in which the self may develop its own "masculine" potentialities or project these onto a hero. Following Carl Jung, let us look at the three basic types of heroes. The extroverted hero of action fights our battles for us (whatever they be) and liberates us (whatever our bondage), changing the structure of society. The introverted hero brings new values and a way of life for us to follow. The third type of hero seeks to transform the personality in order that one might become one's own hero, accomplishing for oneself the tasks of both extroversion and introversion.

Women who today find themselves in the heroic stage appear to be seeking the extroverted hero of action to fight their battles rather than envisioning themselves as heroes.

Now without attempting to draw a one to one correspondence, I would like to look at some representative theories of atonement in the history of Christianity, asking you to keep the three types of heroes in mind. Origin represents the objectivist theories which locate the atonement in the battle between Christ and Satan with Christ being the victor. The event is accomplished outside the self. Abelard represents subjectivists theories. Rather than event outside the self, Jesus' self-sacrificing love calls out a responding love in us. Anselm combines the subjective and the objective, saying that Christ's suffering satisfies God's wrath and insures justice, and yet the self must appropriate the act.

If Christ is the hero accomplishing all in his fighting the battle for us, then we have no need for self-transformation. But if you see Christ either as model calling forth a responding action or as enabling the self-transformation within us, the discussion of salvation in relation to creative transformation will be useful.

Carl Jung says that in the history of all consciousness the hero myth leads into the myth of self transformation, the myth of divine daughter or son. We are moving back to reclaiming self in the image of God.

Salvation as wholeness requires turning in a new direction. However, one must first recognize one's lack. Jung likewise speaks of transformation requiring first a realization of incompleteness. One must move toward reclaiming those aspects of life previously cut off, whether masculine or feminine. I would like to turn now to the feminine archetype in order to talk about the fourth stage of reclaiming the feminine.

I shall be using diagrams developed from Eric Neumann's classic work on the feminine entitled *The Great Mother*. Diagram 1 shows both the matriarchal functions and the anima functions. Anima, meaning soul, is both the archetypal feminine experience and the male's inner feminine potentiality. On the diagram, the "M" axis equals the matriarchal functions and the "A" axis the anima functions. Each function corresponds to a whole sphere of feminine images and modes of being in the world. The move along the axes

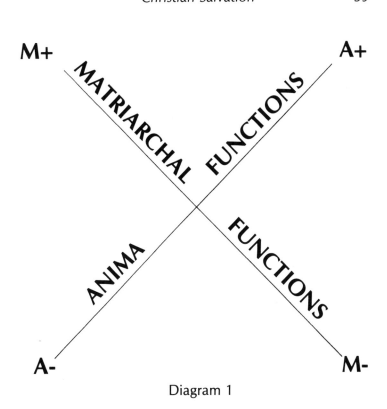

Diagram 1

represent change, unrest, tension, and development toward the goal of creative transformation.

Let us look first at the center, the containing vessel of all life, whether the biological womb or the creative matrix of all culture, whether Mother Earth or the Ground of All Being. (Diagram 2) Women are currently denying this most basic function of the feminine because it has been used all too often to enslave us. It must be reclaimed both as the basis of the mothering function and the anima function before we can be transformed. The return will be different. We now control the use of the vessel rather than being used or denying its existence.

As we move on the A positive and M positive axes, (Diagram 3) that which is contained is released or given

Diagram 2

out. Mythically, Pandora is illustrative of this stage. She, like Eve, is the mother of all living. You have all no doubt heard the expression, "once you have opened Pandora's box." Pandora's box, prior to the Greek adoption of the myth, was an earthen jar, the vessel of all life; in the matriarchal mysteries Pandora poured fourth grain and fruit. However, her box as seen through the eyes of the Greeks contained all the woes of the world—not unlike Eve's being the source of all evil. Pandora is both positive and negative Mother and anima.

Still considering the function of bearing and releasing, let us remember that the matriarchal myths portray the bearing of children in relation to other productive activity. For example, Jane Harrison tells that when women planted maize the stalk was believed to produce more abundantly because the women knew how to bear children. Today's society has yet to see the

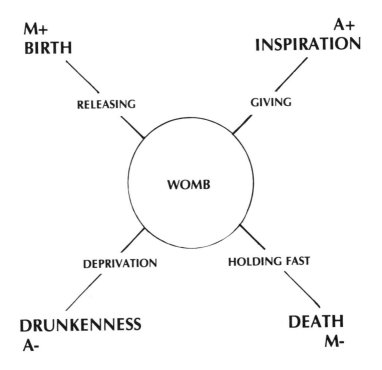

Diagram 3

resources of the mother in terms of the skills acquired which might be useful to a developing society.

Opposite to the function of releasing is that of ensnaring or holding fast. The image here is the black widow spider. On the everyday level, the mother binds the child to herself through her over-protection. The devouring image is seen in numerous fairy tales such as the witch in Hansel and Gretel shoving the children into an oven. The witch imagery begins as the binding or fixating of power in order to control. Power bound into narrow confines will burst asunder. One must learn to use power through releasement.

At the outer ends of the M poles we have birth-death-rebirth phenomena. Romanticism operates along this axis, as in the imagery of fruit ripening, falling to the ground, and returning. On the negative side the terrible mother may represent both death and the possibility of life. Hecate, for example, represents the strength and power of the underworld as witch and mistress of the dead; yet, as moon goddess she is the helper of women giving birth. On the positive end we have the vegetation mysteries of the goddess of grain, Demeter, earth mother. (Diagram 4)

Let us move to the anima pole. All too often even Jungian psychoanalysis presents anima only in terms of the feminine potential in men. But we must keep in mind that the vision also reflects the highest possibilities for the nature of women.

On the positive anima pole the first function is giving. Many of the goddesses were named because of their gifts, such as Sophia's gift of wisdom. Basically the gift of all anima goddesses is the spirit of life itself.

Life as a gift on the positive anima pole stands in opposition to the feeling of deprivation and rejection of the negative anima pole. As an example of negative anima one might consider our present philosophy of existence. Existentialism's main exponents, Martin

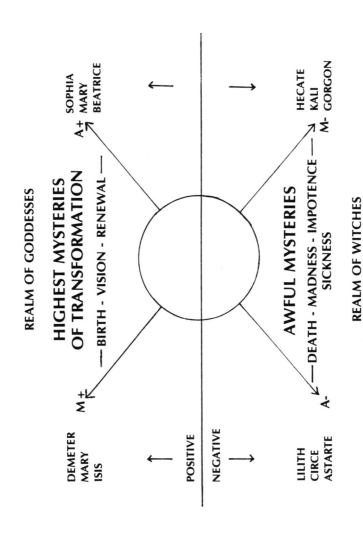

REALM OF GODDESSES

HIGHEST MYSTERIES
OF TRANSFORMATION
—— BIRTH - VISION - RENEWAL ——

A+ SOPHIA
MARY
BEATRICE

M+

DEMETER
MARY
ISIS

POSITIVE

NEGATIVE

AWFUL MYSTERIES
—— DEATH - MADNESS - IMPOTENCE ——
SICKNESS

M– HECATE
KALI
GORGON

A–

LILITH
CIRCE
ASTARTE

REALM OF WITCHES

Diagram 4

Heidegger and Jean Paul Sartre, center on the feeling of being thrown into the world and the subsequent feeling of emptiness. The theme of existential literature might be "you can't go home again." The negative way of anima leads to transformation in the theater of the absurd in our day, to seeing people becoming transformed into beetles and rhinoceroses.

Opposite the negative transformation is positive transformation through sublimation of the instincts. Keep in mind that Freud repeatedly told us that sublimation is not repression. One is not turned into the animal instincts but learns to be at home with them, raising them to another level of creativity. One has only to look at the endless variations of the fairy tales, such as Beauty and the Beast, to see the transformation when the beastial is accepted.

If the beastial is not accepted and one unconsciously becomes the beast, one moved either to madness or to impotence and stupor. Yet at the poles one may easily flip into the opposite. At the furthermost points the poles meet. At the negative anima and the negative mother poles, the psychic spiritual death as well as physical death may be the turning points for resurrection.

Think of the many creative geniuses where madness and genius fuse. There is only the thinnest line between lowered consciousness and raised consciousness. The move between is the source of new vision and creative wisdom. The source of vision and inspiration we call the muse, the source of wisdom, Sophia. This feminine wisdom and vision is that which transforms everyday reality into the depths of universal meaning. We learn to feel at home in the world.

Both the vegetation mysteries and the inspiration mysteries, the Eleusinian mysteries located at the tops of the A and M poles, were connected with the realities of everyday life, not only birth, death and renewal, but also cooking, sewing, eating, cleaning, and weaving. The Eleusinian mysteries made rituals of women's self-consciousness, simultaneously creatively determining the development of human culture. The transformation of self led to the transformation of activities and things.

To see the implication of this making sacred of all events for understanding Christian redemption, I would like to quote Paul Tillich on the nature of revelation: "Revelation is not information about divine things, it is the ecstatic manifestation of the Ground of Being in events, persons, and things. Such manifestations have shaking, transforming, and healing powers." The positive anima function is that of creative transformation. It is the most needed function in the modern world, where life has become all too often empty mechanization of persons, events, and things.

The making sacred of everyday life comes by way of new vision, the Jungian eschatological salvation model. For Jung the dream offers prophetic vision rather than past model. The vision or image comes out of the potentialities of oneself. In Christian terms one talks of the vision of the Kingdom but simultaneously asserts, "The Kingdom is at hand." Jung's vision of wholeness is the fully developed polarities of selfhood, as male-female, anima-animus.

Goddesses as Symbols
of
Feminine Consciousness

"It is not surprising that Psyche's name is the Greek word for Spirit used in the New Testament."

5

Goddesses as Symbols of Feminine Consciousness

The move between stages of consciousness was celebrated in the Eleusinian mysteries in Greece for at least two thousand years before the birth of Jesus.

Again, in order to review woman's transformations of consciousness, I am referring to Erich Neumann's study of "The Psychological Stages of Feminine Development."

The first stage of development is the symbiotic unity with the mother. Here the consciousness of woman is not differentiated from mother consciousness. At this stage one cannot discern a difference between mother and child. Consciousness is undeveloped. On a physical level the child is still embedded in its world. Psychologically, this is the daughter bound to mother; sometimes the binding is never loosened even in the move to a marriage. The marriage may simply be another step in symbiotic union without a differentiation of consciousness. This problem is illustrated in a recent best seller by Nancy Friday, *My Mother, My Self*.

Women are just beginning to face the dilemma of

the negative mother, the mother who cannot let her child go. The woman's movement has been slow in addressing the negative and understandably so in that the major battle at hand is seeking to make visible the positive side of woman. After all, psychologists have never ceased to blame all the ills of humankind on faulty mothering. But this fact may blind us to a problem at hand.

The mother who would allow the daughter to move from this stage must let her daughter go, let her be.

The mythology of the mother who cannot let the daughter go is told in Greece as the story of Demeter, Persephone, and Hekate. It is difficult to tell where daughter begins and where mother ends. Demeter is the mother who cannot accept her daughter's sexuality. When Persephone is abducted into the underworld, Demeter becomes depressed, roams the earth, and loses her function as earth mother, giver of life. Demeter has lost part of herself. She can retrieve it only through the other side of herself, Hekate. To make her own contact with the underworld she sits beside the Virgin Well—marking the entrance between realms. The mother of the earth's surfaces is beginning to get in touch with the depths.

The way to woman's nature leads through a descent into the underworld and a return. It is noteworthy that Hekate, the underground side of the mother, saw the whole thing from her cave. Thus she is depicted in numerous versions of the myth as the torch bearer, lighting the way for the descent and return.

James Hillman in *The Dream and the Underworld* notes the value of Hekate consciousness:

> Hekate was supposedly standing by the whole time, listening or watching. There is evidently a perspective that can witness the soul's struggles without the flap of Persephone or the disaster of

Demeter. It is also a dark angel (Hekate was also called *angelos*), a consciousness (and she was called 'phosphorus') that shines in the dark and that witnesses such events because it already is aware of them a priori . . . . Part of us is not dragged down but always lived there as Hekate is partly an underworld goddess.[1]

Her mode of consciousness is seeing in the dark, seeing through the night. As the goddess who bears the torch and illumines the night, she is the goddess of the moon.

This torch vision in the underworld is a key to the consciousness of woman. She has the insight of the Sibyl, the keeper of the gates of the underworld, the one who can put the broken parts together and enable the return. It is in this sense that she is the goddess of childbirth. Every birth requires a descent to that realm where death and birth lie cheek to jowl.

Strangely enough there is a growing movement of women who consider themselves both witches and theologians. Examples of their views can be found in *Womanspirit Rising*. One of the rituals is the spiral dance which is reminiscent of the dance of the maenads. It is a movement which induces that other mode of seeing, an altered state of consciousness. Perhaps this is the night vision they share with the initiates of the Eleusinian mysteries who imbibed the Soma mentioned in the Vedic hymns. Whatever the cause of the altered state—dance, sexuality, Soma, hallucinogenic mushroom—the consciousness is a seeing from the dark side of the psyche, a consciousness natural to what were once called witches and thus Hekate. Although natural to Hekate the vision in the underworld can be overwhelming.

The frenzied dance of the maenads symbolizes woman overwhelmed by the encounter with the bisexual god, Dionysus. Dionysus had his place in the worship at Eleusis. There he appears in the first stage of consciousness as a divine child cared for by the nurse mother Demeter.

But in the second stage of consciousness Dionysus is experienced as the overpowering or invading masculine God. His abduction of women is the counterpart of Pluto's rape of Persephone into Hades. Dionysus' driving the women into manic frenzy is woman's first stage of encounter with the masculine other or her own masculine potentialities, what Jung calls soul as animus. The fascinating vision of woman's potentialities at this stage are projected onto a male god —hence the designation of Dionysus as the god of women or as having the sexual attributes of female as well as male.

If Dionysus receives the projected potentialities of woman, perhaps the best way to retrieve them is to look to his female counterpart Ariadne.

Ariadne is abducted, like Persephone, by Theseus and abandoned on an island. Dionysus runs a parallel course with the human male Theseus, although some versions of the myth say he rescued Ariadne from her abandonment by Theseus. Nevertheless it appears that Dionysus also abandoned her before she could bring his child to birth.

Ariadne is that woman who combined two modes of seeing—the technical knowledge of how the maze of the underworld was constructed with the imaginative vision or the ability to see in the dark. Her thread was woven from the flax of the master craftsman Daedalus and the thread of the imaginative vision of the dark god.

According to Walter Otto in *Dionysus: Myth and Cult*, the myths of Ariadne alternate between the extremes of sorrow and joy, making him wonder whether two goddesses were involved.[2] I suggest rather that the psychological dynamics are the archetypal basis for the manic/depressive swings of extreme ecstasy and depression. The powers of perception open to the depths of the underworld or unconscious enable seeing through the maze of the unconscious, understanding how all the fragments fit the pattern. But the wholistic vision so overwhelms, seduces, and fascinates that it is extremely difficult to bring it to conscious birth. Perhaps the men who tried to finish the birth cries of Ariadne understood what she was trying to bring into being.

When the total darkness is illumined from below, to give birth through the pupil causes blindness. Ariadne's thread could lead others through but she had to remain in the dark.

Psyche, like Ariadne, was married to a dark god. Given to this god by her father, Psyche was involved in a patriarchal marriage of the second stage of consciousness. She lived in the castle with the beast and was under his command never to look upon him but only to lie with him in the night. At the prodding of her sisters she dared to light a candle and look upon the beast. They enable Psyche to see her situation in a new light, marking a turning point in the development of the feminine psyche. Holding the light before the face of the god, Psyche drops hot wax on the sleeping Eros. Angry at her defiance, he flees home to Momma. Psyche, on the other hand, is freed to begin her own quest of psychic development and the quest for an unveiled relationship to the god.

Psyche is given the tasks of the hero. First, she is to sort out a pile of seeds into their proper categories, a task suggesting a confrontation with male sexuality. Her second task is to bring golden fleece back from the rams, suggesting a confrontation with male aggression. She learns not to charge head on but wait until the sun goes down and pick the fleece left in the thicket. Psyche has to encompass the power of the masculine without being shattered by it. Her third task is to fill a vessel with water from the rivers of the underworld, suggesting a journey to the unconscious. She herself becomes the vessel. The final task is a trip to the underworld to bring back the treasure of beauty for Aphrodite. Here the task ends when Psyche takes as her own the attributes of the Mother Goddess. Through the developed consciousness of herself as hero and through her awareness of the two sides of the beast, she liberates Eros from Aphrodite. Because of her ego consciousness, she could withstand the descent into the underworld and return. In her pregnancy she reunites with the maternal feminine, but not regressively, marking the move to the fourth stage of feminine consciousness. Psyche is raised to Mt. Olympus and gives birth to a divine daughter called Pleasure.

It is not surprising that Psyche's name is the Greek word for Spirit used in the New Testament.

Notes

1. James Hillman, *The Dream and the Underworld* (New York: Harper & Row, 1979), pp. 49-50.
2. Walter Otto, *Dionysus: Myth and Cult* (Bloomington and London: Indiana University Press, 1965), p. 188.

Spirit "as" Feminine Consciousness

"And it is through the depths of our own psyche that Spirit lets itself be seen or heard. This is the creative dynamic of the feminine spirit."

6

Spirit "as" Feminine Consciousness

The basic thesis of this chapter is that we are entering a new stage or mode of consciousness.

Recall that according to Jung the heroic stage followed the patriarchal stage of consciousness. The theological correlate is that, following death of God theology, the "Radical" theologians proclaimed the religion of the Son: the father God died in our time in order to become incarnate in the flesh of Jesus. Freud would refer to this move as killing the father in order to have a religion of the brothers. But in our post-radical theology something new is emerging.

Jung said that beyond the heroic stage of consciousness appears the appropriation of the feminine spirit. Beyond the religion of the Son is the religion of Spirit. In John 16:6-7 we hear the words: "It is to your advantage that I go away, for if I do not go away the Spirit will not come to you."

Following the stage of Jesus as hero fighting the battles of atonement and reconciliation for the individual, one must appropriate her/his own potentialities for heroism. If Jesus as God incarnate goes away in order that Spirit may enliven each individual, then the next step in the transformation of human consciousness is a religion of the Spirit as God dwelling through human beings. The question is how to open toward this dimension of God.

I am following the correlation method of Paul Tillich. What is changing in the existential human situation that may open symbols to the Spiritual presence? Clearly the most radical change in present society is emerging feminine consciousness. Although it runs the same risk of objectivization as does Spirit, I wish to explore a possible correlation between the transformation of feminine consciousness and the changing Spirit consciousness.

First a word on the Holy Spirit and then on Feminine spirit. I find it instructive that we have in practice a binitarian rather than a trinitarian theology. We have yet to fully develop the doctrine of Spirit. The question is why? Could it be that the Spirit dimension of the Godhead contains the truncated female imagery?

Because Spirit is that manifestation of God presently in the world, I believe the search for feminine imagery should be sought through the Spirit. We cannot arbitrarily change the fact that the father metaphor functioned for the Hebrew people nor the fact that Jesus was male. We can seek new metaphors for the way in which God relates to women and men today.

Let us first seek to understand Spirit through some representative Biblical references. I would call to your attention that the Old Testament word for spirit, "ruach" is feminine gender, as is the New Testament word "psyche." And the other major New Testament word for spirit, "pneuma" is neuter. I do not wish to claim that Spirit is feminine on the basis of word gender, but I do wish to understand the Spirit in terms of the dynamics of the feminine archetype.

In Genesis 1 we read that "the Spirit of God was brooding over the face of the waters," present at the beginning of all creation. Here the Spirit is in some way connected with creation by the word, "and God said." In Psalms 33:6, God's creating by the breath or spirit is paralleled by the word of God. One of the tests for canonization of scripture was inspiration by the Spirit. The prophet's words were gifts of the Spirit.

Recall that the dynamics of positive anima involve the appropriation of feminine consciousness as the basis for inspiration whether for the creative poetic or prophetic word.

As the people are filled with the Spirit at Pentecost they move to another form of consciousness, speaking in other tongues. Ecstatic utterance is followed by the structured word, as Peter begins to preach: "And in the last days it shall be, God declares, that I will pour out my Spirit upon all flesh and your sons and your daughters shall prophesy . . . ."

In addition to inspiration of the word, Spirit follows the dynamics of the feminine as creative transformation. In Isaiah 32, we read that the Spirit of God transforms the desert and makes it an abode of justice. In Psalms 51, the Spirit is the creative transforming power bringing forth new spirit.

The highest form of feminine spirit, according to Carl Jung, is wisdom or Sophia. In Proverbs 8 it is feminine wisdom who is present in the beginning of all creation, paralleling the Spirit brooding over the waters in Genesis.

> Does not Wisdom call?
> Does not understanding raise her voice?
> . . . I, Wisdom, am mistress of discretion,
> the inventor of lucidity of thought.
> Good advice and sound judgement belong to me.
> . . . by me rulers govern,

and the great impose justice on the world.
From everlasting I was firmly set,
from the beginning, before earth came into being.
The deep was not, when I was born;
there were no springs to gush with water.
Before the mountains were settled,
before the hills, I came to birth.
. . . When Yahweh laid down the foundations of
     the earth
I was alongside, a living bond
bringing delight day after day
ever at play in the world.

The place of Spirit as feminine wisdom has yet to be developed in Christian theology. Carl Jung writes that the female element in the diety is covered over, with the interpretation of the Holy Spirit as Sophia being considered heretical.

Let us step back from our discussion of Spirit and seek to understand the feminine figure of Wisdom personified as Sophia. To understand her dynamics, I need once again to summarize the developmental stages of the feminine psyche.

In the matriarchal phase, both male and female are contained in the great round, but the ego is not yet differentiated. The move to the patriarchy is necessary as the female becomes aware of the masculine as other and of her own instinctual nature. At this stage she lives out the father's anima or image of femininity. In the third stage she looks to a hero, either a husband or at best a female authority figure (role model), for rescue from the father. In either case her own "masculine" potentialities are projected. The task is to move to realize them within herself. But, even so, one is still striving to realize masculine values, and very often at this third stage feminine values are denied by both male and female. The fourth stage is the reincorporation of the original feminine values of the matriarchal stage but at a level of the developed consciousness of an Athena or a Deborah.

The good mother—whose work included both the creation of children and culture—will appear again when she no longer has to do with an embryonic ego, but with a self-conscious adult personality. She reveals herself at this final stage as Sophia, feminine spirit incorporated into the everyday realities of life.

Imagine the circle of the feminine archetype. Wherever you start, when you come full circle, the end will also be the beginning. One of the most difficult problems in understanding feminine development is to know when the return to mother is regressive and when it marks the highest development incorporating feminine spirit. It is the totality of the archetype which must be affirmed for wholeness of selfhood. When we come full circle perhaps the metaphor of spiritual mother as Sophia will have renewed meaning.

Sophia is the mother who gives birth to logos, in her archetypal dimension. The anima component of the personality is connected with the voice, the creative element in the individual. Positive anima is the basis of both prophetic and poetic word.

The symbolic figure of Sophia stands at the beginning of the highest development of human spirit or psyche, according to Jung. And it is through the depths of our own psyche that Spirit lets itself be seen or heard. This is the creative dynamic of the feminine spirit.

When psyche retrieves the treasure from the depths, the question is how to bring it back to life. How does one talk about the encounter with God as Spirit; how does one put it into language without remaking the subject object or the object subject?

Sophia and the Clown

"The problem with interpretation is that both the mother and the counterpart are double-sided—there is the positive Mary Sophia, queen of heaven, and her dying son, the Christ; but on the other side is the underworld Chthonic mother who appears with Hermes, the twin who is both trickster and the god of revelation, messenger of the gods, the Hermes of Hermeneutics."

7

Sophia and the Clown

One way to talk about the encounter with the God(s) is through the symbolic language of images which appear in dreams, visions, or the stage between, waking dreams.

The waking dream which I call Sophia and the Clown appeared seven years ago. At the time I had never read about the Greek gods and goddesses nor had I ever read the psychology of Carl Jung. Nevertheless, in the time since, I have found incredible parallels from both sources which help me begin to decipher the images. The method of dream interpretation is best explained as a treasure hunt. Originally the picture was simply enacted. I wrote it down and over the years as I chanced upon or searched for clues I went back to the dream for new insight. On one occasion I said the dream was complete, and I intended to drop it. Not long thereafter I recalled another entire scene, left out of my work on the dream, for a consultation on dreams and revelation.

Scene one, originally forgotten, was the seeing of the word "odea" written out in negative space surrounded by black background. Since I did not know

Greek, the word remained a puzzle. I finally discovered that it was the plural of "odeum," in Ancient Greece a roofed building for musical and dramatic performances; hence, it is related to the word "ode." The recollection and subsequent discovery shed new light on the second scene (originally taken to be the first).

Scene two was the seeing of the word "eidos" written out again in open space emerging out of the dark background. In looking for the meaning of "ode," I discovered "-ode," a suffix denoting a thing that is like, from French, "eidos." The Greeks called the appearance of a thing "eidos." Prior to the recall of scene one, I had sought to understand "eidos" through word association, moving from "eidos" to idol. *Webster's New World Dictionary* lists the roots of the word "idol" as "eidolon" meaning an image and "eidos" meaning form. Hence I recalled Plato's forms as "eidos." The definition of "idol" is an image of god which appears as a shadow or an image in a mirror. The obsolete meaning (but useful for scene three) is effigy or an image of a person who is despised or held in contempt. Kittel in his article on "eidos" in *The Theological Dictionary of the New Testament* writes that "eidos" means "what is visible," "an appearance." It is also the word used in place of saying the word naming God. For example, Kittel cites John 5:37: "And the Father who sent me has himself borne witness to me. His voice you have never heard, his form ("eidos") you have never seen." Next Kittel refers to the Hebrew word corresponding to "eidos," saying

> Cf. Ex. 41, 3: "Two things Israel asked of God: to see his form (Hebrew equivalent of 'eidos') and to hear the words from His mouth." It is most significant for the position of the Rabbinic exegete that in S. Nu., 103 on 12:8, the explanatory (Hebrew word for 'seeing') is not linked with the I of

God contained in the (Hebrew word for 'word') but is understood as the seeing of speech. Or perhaps the Shekinah? This is correct, for it is written: "And he said, Thou canst not see my face: for there shall no man see me, and live" (Exodus 33:20).

As I understand this, the seeing of saying is the vision or appearance which takes the place of seeing God face to face. The prophets did not hear the saying or word of God but they saw the saying. That which appears in place of God is called Shekinah. Hence, the next step of my treasure hunt was to seek this new word.

Gershom Scholem in *On the Kabbalah and Its Symbolism* says of the Shekinah: "God's presence, what in the Bible is called His face, is in Rabbinical usage, his Shekinah. The word is not found in the Old Testament but is used in later Jewish interpretation and literature as a way of talking about the presence of God without materializing God. According to the Hastings *Dictionary of the Bible* the "Shekinah" means "that which dwells or dwelling." In *The Interpreter's Dictionary of the Bible* it is noted that the Shekinah refers to the place where God dwells with people and gives a name. A.E. Waite in *The Holy Kabbalah* relates the Shekinah to the Tetragrammaton. "She is to God that which the vowel point is to the letter—a thing not distinct therefrom but the means of its utterance."[1] According to the *Encyclopedia Judaica* the Shekinah represents the feminine principle in the divine world. And the highest goal of religion, according to the teachings of the *Kabbalah*, is the reuniting of the masculine and the feminine elements of the Godhead. Also in the *Kabbalah* the Shekinah is called the daughter of a voice. The mystical branch of Jews believed the Shekinah would return with the Messiah.

Gershom Scholem notes that as the Feminine aspect of the divine the Shekinah had its positive and terrible aspects. In her terrible aspects she is the Tree of Death as opposed to the Tree of life. When her "face is dark" she is the vehicle of punishment and judgment. She is both "lower and upper mother," according to the teachings of Kabbalah.[2]

Perhaps now the stage has been set for the move to scene three.

Scene three: I am somewhere between sleeping and waking. Partly dazed from sleep, I looked out from a pre-cut slab concrete apartment through a picture window overlooking the asphalt parking lot to a small oasis containing a clump of pine trees on the left and an oak tree on the right. The oak appeared as a woman, towering to the sky, blood surging up through the veins of bark, a large woman's head emerging from the top, angrily hurling a ball (or celestial orb or ring) with her limbs to the left. Following the wind of her branches, I saw the pines as if asleep, their needles gently floating toward the earth, caught softly in the breeze. In front of the largest pine tree the ring was suspended on the branch about midway between earth and sky. A clown's head hanged from the top of the circle as the ring ceased to turn.

Following the dream, I immediately recalled the movie at the 1966 world's fair entitled *The Parable* in which Christ is the despised and rejected clown. But why does the woman throw the ball that hanged him? In the movie the clown was black, and whites were throwing balls that made him fall into a tub of water. Could the clown suggest the encounter with the shadow? Could the woman be rejecting her shadow and projecting it onto the clown/Christ? The dream has never made complete sense to me although it continues to energize my imagination. Its fascination has led me into a long search to understand the symbols.

Let us begin with the tree. I later read Mircea Eliade's *The Sacred and the Profane* and discovered that the sacred shows itself through ordinary objects such as stones or trees. Trees, like mountains and ladders, indicate a movement between two realms. I thought of Jacob's ladder marking the place where a confrontation between heaven and earth took place. One assumes there must have been anger when Jacob wrestled with his angel.

Eliade writes in *Images and Symbols* that it is quite archaic to find the cosmic tree with entrances to hell, earth and heaven as a symbol of the center.

In *Man and His Symbols* Jung tells of a child's dream showing the ancient symbolism of the dying god and its relation to the Great Mother symbolized by the tree. In his study of the Great Mother archetype he says she always appears paired with her counterpart. The problem with this interpretation is that both the mother and the counterpart are double sided—there is the positive Mary Sophia, queen of heaven, and her dying son, the Christ; but on the other side is the underworld Chthonic mother who appears with Hermes, the twin who is both trickster and the god of revelation, messenger of the gods, the Hermes of "Hermeneutics."

Like the move between "idol" and that which appears as God, the seeing of saying, so the move between the giant woman emerging from the trunk of the tree to the heights of the sky and the clown on the rung hanged midway between earth and sky poses the question which side is appearing. Or are both appearing simultaneously?

Again I can only return to the concrete symbols. The tree out of which the woman emerges is an oak tree. Jung says in his alchemical studies that the oak tree was the central figure among the contents of the unconscious, possessing personality in the most marked degree, yet the core was still hidden in the oak, asleep.

The oak is the prototype of the self, a symbol of the source and the goal of the individuation process.[3]

I find it noteworthy that since dreaming the dream or the dream dreaming me, I have begun to notice women using the tree as a symbol of their emerging selfhood. If the tree is the emerging selfhood of woman evoking the presence of the Mother goddess, then the question again is why is she so angry with what appears to me through the double faced clown as Christ and Hermes? I do not fully comprehend, but it keeps hitting me that out of the deep psyche of woman there is a realization that the Mother, as well as the Father, has to sacrifice the Son in order to free the spirit. But more I cannot yet say.

Sometimes one becomes so attached to an image that one cannot preside over its death. This is where Hermes frees one for interpretation.

For the alchemist the spirit Mercurius or Hermes was to be found confined only in the oak tree. Hermes, in his dual nature, as evil spirit lies hidden in the roots of the tree but when raised from the earth through the mother is cleansed and changed into spirit (wind).[4] After the ascension as spirit he descends to earth again.[5] It is as if the movement of his opposite side were reversed, seen in a mirror. Christ descended, died, ascended, and the spirit was freed. Hermes ascended, spirit was freed, then descended. Jung does not say he died as a way of descending, but he does note that Hermes' archetype is the trickster, often seen as clown.[6]

In my vision the clown hung midway between heaven and earth.

Jung says that the alchemists saw Mercurius or Hermes as the second Adam, the mediator between heaven and earth.[7] Hermes was the messenger between gods and persons. He is the shadow or counterpart of Christ, what the alchemists called ''God's reflection in physical nature.''

The source of the dual nature of Hermes arose out of the split between conscious and unconscious, according to Jung, and was projected in theology as the split between the forces of light and dark.[8] The split came as the alchemists worked to free spirit from matter. The goal was the philosopher's tree or stone, the freeing of ''the world creating spirit of God from the chains of Physis.''[9] Specifically, the tree was marked by a life renewing system of blood vessels.[10]

When Hermes is released two ways of seeing are possible, seeing as light or seeing as dark, good or evil. Hermes foreshadowed the light but was not the light.[11] For those who cannot ''see'' the light, Hermes becomes the diabolical seducer. The two ways of seeing correspond to the conscious and unconscious modes of perception. Jung says the clown is the trickster, understood psychologically as the picture which primitive consciousness formed of itself.[12] The trickster ''in his clearest manifestation . . . is a faithful reflection of an absolutely undifferentiated human consciousness. Considering the crude primitivity of the trickster cycle, it would not be surprising if one saw in this myth simply the reflection of an earlier, rudimentary stage of consciousness, which is what the trickster seems to be.''[13] In the case of the trickster a higher level of consciousness has covered up a lower level. To uncover is not to lose the shadow but rather its fascination.[14]

Jung concludes that the clown is the remnant of the collective shadow. If the trickster hints at a saviour, the vision shows that out of our fascination with the dark side, the collective shadow, may come hope.[15] But first we must lose our fascination with the negative. By negative I mean that reverse image which precedes the picture; the opposites of light and dark switch between the negative and the processed image. It is simply an earlier stage of developing, a more primitive image.

The clown hung as a ball from an evergreen, the

"tree of life."[16] The clown hung over the circus ring as a hanged god from a pine tree, the tree of Dionysus, god of the mask.[17]

Samuel H. Miller, in an essay entitled "The Clown in Contemporary Art" refers to the clown as "the man with two shadows, the fool, the failure—the other in the sky, incredibly gay, utterly impossible but never unbelievable, where the bright banners of his lonely dreams and shy hopes fly in the heroic winds of a very human heaven."[18]

If the clown is indeed the man of two shadows, then the woman emerging from the oak was casting out her double shadow. Erich Neumann calls the stage of "a woman without a shadow" the counterpart of woman's false identification with Sophia, the Spirit Mother who corresponds to the Spirit Father.[19] It is false not because woman does not have the potential of Sophia but because her consciousness is not yet developed to be able to incarnate that which is trying to come to appearance.

Notes

1. A.E. Waite, *The Holy Kabbalah* (New York: Macmillan, 1929), p. 345.
2. Gershom Scholem, *On the Kabbalah and Its Symbolism*, trans. Ralph Manheim (London: Routledge and Kegan Paul, 1965), p. 107.
3. C.G. Jung, *Alchemical Studies: The Collected Works of C.G. Jung*, eds. Herbert Read, Michael Fordham, Gerbard Adler, William McGuire, trans. R.F.C. Hall (Bollingen Series XX; Princeton, N.J.: Princeton University Press, 1967), p. 194.
4. Jung, p. 231.
5. Jung, p. 233.
6. C.G. Jung, *Four Archetypes: Mother, Rebirth, Spirit, Trickster*, trans. R.F.C. Hall (London: Routledge and Kegan Paul, 1972), p. 142.

7. Jung, *Alchemical Studies*, p. 235.

8. Jung, *Alchemical Studies*, p. 243.

9. Jung, *Alchemical Studies*, p. 307.

10. Jung, *Alchemical Studies*, p. 287.

11. Jung, *Alchemical Studies*, p. 248.

12. Jung, *Four Archetypes*, p. 141.

13. Jung, *Four Archetypes*, p. 141.

14. Jung, *Four Archetypes*, p. 144.

15. Jung, *Four Archetypes*, pp. 151-152.

16. C.G. Jung, *Man and His Symbols* (New York: Dell Publishing Co., 1964), p. 69.

17. Walter Otto, *Dionysus: Myth and Cult* (Bloomington and London: Indiana University Press, 1965), Ch. 6.

18. Samuel H. Miller, "The Clown in Contemporary Art," *Theology Today*, Vol. 24, 1967, p. 328.

19. Erich Neumann, "The Psychological Stages of Feminine Development," *Spring*, trans. Rebecca Jackson, rev. Hildegard Nagel and Jane Pratt (New York: The Analytical Psychology Club, 1959), p. 74.

Imaginal Consciousness:
The Bridge Between

"The question which continued for some time in my dream series was how to get across to the other side before the bridge is constructed in order to see how it should be built."

8

Imaginal Consciousness:
The Bridge Between

Imagination transforms the bridge between two thresholds of consciousness, two ways of seeing. The dream is a primary way of bringing the image to view, a vehicle that lets one see two banks, the self stretched between, and the way across.

Construction under the bridge became visible in a dream of a turning. Fortune grabbed the wheel of my automobile and turned it around and into the center of the first loop of a cloverleaf leading down off the superhighway. At the intersection of the cloverleaf I met the brother of the Buddha with head over heels, hands clasped around knees, rolling round and round and rocking backward and forward, saying and laughing: "Knowledge is knowing what you do not know. Know not you . . . ." Each turn took him closer to the middle and another level deeper. My dream self stood in the shadow thinking he did not know what he was talking about. And I awakened laughing.

A few nights later I dreamed that my self was a tree stretched between two sections of interstate highways.

The first half of the tree was carved revealing the self image hidden within the deeper rings of the tree. As I saw beneath the bridge through the underlayers of concentric circles of cloverleafs, the wood shavings carved themselves off the top of the tree and spiraled upward as the cloverleafs spiraled downward to form a bridge beneath the bridge. On the surface there was a saw horse at the end of the constructed section of the road bridge saying: "Stop: Bridge Under Construction."

The question which continued for some time in my dream series was how to get across to the other side before the bridge is constructed in order to see how it should be built.

First, I went the bottom way. Realizing that the downward spiral of cloverloops was endless, I went to the space where the flow of the river and the wind came together to create a rhythmic movement that held all the bridge posts together by the backward and forward flow. This was the level of tree roots that flow all the way across the river.

There I tried to ride a tree across the bottom as a "tree stick," having roots as broom straw, with a hollow for carrying others across. I kept having pity on the three hurt dogs who appeared along the bottom. Each time I turned and carried them back to the other side. Something told me they would die on the side I was headed toward. On awakening I recalled the three-headed dog that guarded the access to the other side when crossing the River Styx.

The question still remained: how does one cross before the bridge is finished? Next I tried the way across the heights. I was trying to learn to fly as well as ride in a supersonic vision plane. But in the dream the heights needed to come together with the depths. When it landed I could see through the water beneath the tree to a black pearl—but it could not yet be retrieved.

Finally, I just awakened one morning and realized

that in the night I had reached the far side and that roads were already there rising to meet my steps in the water which hid the roads. I could not decide whether to take the tree raft formed of a communion of carving selves along. I knew I had crossed on the raft; but having tried to carry it, I also saw that the weight was too much if I wished to go further. I decided to trust the tracks beneath my feet, although covered with water, and let the raft float back to the bank. If the water became too deep I knew I could look for a tree or at least a stick. Then I awakened.

The immediate context of dreaming the last dream was the struggle to write this book on imaginal consciousness in which I wanted to draw the bridge between a number of doubles: the double self, double vision, the double brain, double consciousness, and hermeneutics as a backward and forward movement.

The problem in writing this book, in freeing my own imagination, is the raft on which I cross. Thinking that the raft itself is the subject matter makes putting all the trees together cumbersome. Some of those exquisitely carved trees that came together for me through the dream were my first encounter at a level of insight with Zen Buddhism; my chance reading of a young man of imaginative genius, Douglas Hofstadter, in a work entitled *Godel, Escher, Bach: The Eternal Golden Braid*; Julian Jaynes' *The Origin of Consciousness in the Breakdown of the Bicameral Mind*; Martin Heidegger's seeing ''something as something;'' Wittgenstein's ''seeing as;'' the seers, those prophets who saw the saying of the God; Carl Jung's mandalas, Ezekiel's wheel within the wheel in the middle of the earth, Rodin's and Michelangelo's sculptures, and finally Paul Ricoeur's *Freud and Philosophy: An Essay in In-*

terpretation—especially his archeological and teleological hermeneutics as a base for understanding the backward and forward movement of the imagination.

To carve each tree would yield the raft but to do this on a rational analytic level would require an entire series of volumes on the imagination and that is the problem. It is the task of imaginal consciousness, the bridge between hemispheres, to be able to take endless sense data input, rearrange, condense, and finally transform the pluralism, the multiplicity, into an image which contains it all *if one only learns to see*.

What is needed is not yet another interpretation. What is needed is *to see!* We can interpret dreams so much that we fail to see what is given as clearly as our consciousness can give it. At issue for dream hermeneutics, and especially for Biblical hermeneutics, is whether we need a more sophisticated decoding system or whether we need eyes to see.

Let me say it again. I think we have taken a wrong turn. We have assumed that the subject was the scripture, the creed, the doctrine, etc. and that our task for interpretation, if only we could get our hermeneutics straight, was to decipher what was really said, what really happened, what the parable really meant. What if Jesus meant for us to throw away the stories once we had seen, and learn to tell new parables from what is at hand? The raft is heavy.

Fooling Around:
The Soul of Wisdom

"Dorothy in search of a brain for her friend the straw man is given a doctorate in thinkology. In search of wisdom, behind the clown mask, I received a doctorate in foolishness, mirth, a-muse."

9

Fooling Around:
The Soul of Wisdom

When I was seeking publication of my first article, an editor advised me to become more self-conscious of my methodology. Taking his advice, I read back through what I had written and deduced that I was reading only the *images* in the texts of Martin Heidegger. I now recognize that I was reading Heidegger's thought from a right hemisphere perspective. This was possible because the right was latent in the work as its foundation. The right hemisphere of the brain sees in images while the left sees in language. The image is the stuff of myth—what Heidegger calls the preunderstanding. Right hemisphere perceives the whole through a reversal of figure and ground, what the artist calls seeing the negative space "as" the positive.

The left hemisphere of the brain sees in parts, reasons sequentially, and is ordered by temporality. Since time is in the hemisphere's structure as the condition for the possibility of being in the world, Heidegger could pose the question of *Being* only through *Time*. But if a reversal or a movement from the left hemishere to the right were to occur then time would no longer be the essence of being in the world.

Instead, if right hemisphere perception takes over, figure and ground reverse and the spatial ground itself emerges as the subject matter. Right hemisphere reasoning sees the world as image or picture, sees circumspectly rather than linearly.

Now I need to be clear that I am not writing a book about Heidegger's turn, but rather I am seeing the move between two modes of consciousness as they parallel the two brain hemispheres.

Here my mind doubles or splits, depending upon your perspective.

I need to read backward once again and become conscious of my own right hemisphere methodology in the last two chapters. In so doing I hope to see the way of imaginal consciousness.

In rereading again through "Sophia and the Clown" and "Imaginal Consciousness," it hit me that what I was really doing was simply fooling around. The dialectical need to become serious hit simultaneously, hence the interlude on Heidegger.

Realizing that one major methodological issue was the move between image and language, I began to play with etymology. (Alongside I wondered whether Heidegger played from the other direction and thus incurred all those criticisms about his incorrect etymologies.)

Making fun of those thinkers who find "being" in language, I facetiously looked up "fooling" and "around" in *Webster's Third New International Dictionary*.

"Fool"   "to act or work tentatively or unsystematically—often used with around."

"Around" (fr. a + round), "in a circle or in a circumference: Round (the wheel kept going) . . . .

> from beginning to end . . . . somewhere
> close by: in the vicinity or neighborhood:
> nearby . . . . in the reverse or opposite direc-
> tion: to the rear (suddenly he turned): from
> one opinion, belief, or point of view to an-
> other . . . . in all directions outward from
> . . . . so as to have a center . . . .

I am indeed seriously fooling around.

My epistemology coincides with my changing self-consciousness. I keep seeing double in my dream. To carry the absurd still further, I checked Webster on 'doubling.'

'Doubling' ''The act or process of one that doubles: as (a): a sudden unexpected turn (b): the process of redistilling spirits . . . . (d): the process of plying two or more yarns.

I must confess my first turn (on) toward language but not seriously. My mind laughs: animus/animuse!

I could twine endlessly around these loops, a-muse-ing myself but . . . . (The serious intrudes: women never get published if they aren't taken serious-ly. Perhaps that is what kills the clown/Christ/Hermes . . . animus/e in woman).

While trying to get serious, I recalled an early dream of my car driving up to one side of a gas pump and, after it was filled, quickly speeding down the superhighway. Simultaneously, an exhausted horse lay down on the other side of the pump. No gas was put in and he moved to the other side, showing some renewal of energy as he joined my St. Bernard dog and my golden retriever. I awakened and immediately realized the wrong kind of horse power had been used to fill the spirit—recalling Kierkegaard's spirited horse juxtaposed with Plato's two horses (spirit and instinct) pulling in opposite directions with reason as the charioteer trying to let spirit take the lead while curbing instinct.

It is beginning to dawn on me that imagination as the charioteer lets the self double rather than split . . . . embodying mind/spirit, enspiriting mind/body.

Musing between dream image and language:

"Animate"   (fr. L. *animatus*, past part of *animare* to quicken, enliven, endow with breath or soul, . . . L *animus* soul, mind.) Webster

Animus: The soul of woman projected first onto a father figure and then onto a substitute male hero and then retrieved into herself as her split off masculine other . . . . The move beyond the split must come with seeing both sides as part of the whole but with a developed ego. The differentiation is not lost in the return to wholeness. But first one must unmask one's projections, according to Freud, and then use the projections as the building blocks for moving forward, as Jung suggests. Actually it goes both ways when double consciousness occurs. Unmasking the projections is seeing through the Dionysian mask, the backward movement. The complement is seeing the pattern and thus knowing how to move forward.

————————————

Now I need to back up and see how I got where I am. I am in a dream retracing a path I have been before and move between rooms to try on two dresses, one red and one red and blue plaid squares. I decide to send them with an artistic weaver and her children to the owner who left them behind and move on. The next stop is at a john (head) where the toilet bowl water is running over. The water is clean and through the water

I began to see the pattern of the brown bricks marking the path. My soul guides helped me cut the water back at the source so as to continue to flow but not to cover the path. At this point consciously I realized the pattern of the "yellow" brick road, cluing me to Dorothy's quest to see the Wizard. The fairy tale becomes a bridge.

I then follow the brown brick road to Trafalgar Square where the road circles the square. I take a sharp turn across the brown brick road to the left side. There I see a golden dress entwined with ivy. The dress is on a manikin, i.e., a woman form without a head. (In German, the word "manikin *Mannchen*" means a little man, or a dwarf, i.e., a being who is a child or an old wizened man.) I notice that the manikin in the golden and ivy dress is in front of, and blocking, the entrance to a building facing the square circle.

Before moving to the other side I need to interrupt the dream and ask what these symbols mean. This need comes from realizing that squaring the circle, the reverse image of circling the square, is to make the unconscious conscious.

First the turn. Whenever one changes one's mind, whenever consciousness turns, one has an opportunity to catch a glimpse of where one has been, where one is going and which way one did not turn. It is in this "between" that one may catch a glimpse of both sides of one's mind simultaneously.

Now a look at the dress which turned my head. The ivy is mythologically Dionysus's flower, and the gold is Apollo's. But the question, if these are the masks of woman's animus, is how does she retrieve the gold and the green as her own. Persephone was abducted by Hades or Dionysus and must live underground part of the year, but she, like the ivy, returns to life. The next recollection in interpretation is that the National Gallery was in Trafalgar Square, as was a chapel. I do not recall where they were in the circle. I only passed through briefly on a tour of the continent several years ago. The Gallery clues me to the place of the work of art. My first association is Wallace Stevens' poem "The Rock" where ivy covering the rock is the mask that lets us see, much like *The Anecdote on the Jar*. I then recall a student recently passing on to me W.B. Yeats' poem *The Mask* with the lines: "Put off that mask of burning gold with emerald eyes . . . . It was the mask engaged your mind, And after set your heart to beat, Not what's behind." The fascination with the mask keeps us from seeing the face looking through the mask from behind, woman's animus. Women who cannot let go their fascination with the Dionysian masks are the maenads, women who lose their head in pursuit of Dionysus. The woman without a head recalls that Dorothy's quest included a brain for the straw man from the wizard.

The fascination is in the transference of woman's own animus or soul onto the mask. Fascination, rather than unmasking, can be death for the woman's emerging mode of consciousness.

Women are taught by men who are running the course backward. They begin where she ends, hence her projected goal. Men who are on a quest to rid themselves of one-sided left hemisphere consciousness often make followers of those women who reflect their goal. Woman, so long taught by left hemisphere men, becomes enthralled, enchanted, by the rare man moving toward her so he can find her depths reflected back toward him. The problem is deeper than narcissism. The last test for Dorothy was to unmask the wizard and avoid his invitation for a balloon trip, an inflation leading to flying off into fantasy land forever. The brown brick road lay on the left in the dream, the balloon and helium on the right.

The question of how to retrieve the gold from the mask still remains. One could imagine the brown bricks being transformed into gold bricks but this is still the side of fantasy. The brown earth brick suffices to show the way, even if within a dream. Suddenly the dream begins to move itself into waking dreams and a pile of green garden peas appear. Can one imagine anything any more ordinary and blah? What can one do with peas? It takes a real magician to disguise them, so I start to peel them one by one.

Suddenly the green-covered bronze statue of Lord Nelson, actually in the center of the Square, appeared in a split second with the black pearl beneath the green garden pea.

Now the inter-looping second ply of the yarn became conscious. Psyche's first task was to sort a pile of seeds. Her second task was to fetch a vase of water from the source of the underground river Styx. An eagle helped her. I recalled that in my first view of the pearl, I flew from the heights to the depths in a supersonic vision plane; eagle-eyed vision. Also in that dream, left out in my earlier telling, was the presence in the opposite section of the plane of a King at a round cocktail table. Hence the third ply of the yarn, the third loop of the quest joins the other two.

The journey before I took the turn into the center and encountered Buddha nature, I had been walking down a dry river bed for a long time. It ended with an encounter with a "Fishy" President. I was asked to write the dying man's epitaph. Instead I turned and the river filled with clear water and fish. The quest for the holy grail merges with Psyche's trip to bring back the vase of water from the source of the river Styx. The water of life is in the river of death.

Now I need to put a pattern together and try to

see how these images came together in the unconscious. Lord Nelson is a hero of war, King Arthur
was a hero of war. Psyche was in a quest to become her
own hero. The task for woman at the third stage of consciousness is to develop her own animus characteristics
rather than to project them onto a male hero. The task is
to bring them back from the other side of consciousness.
Dorothy sought a brain for the straw man; followers of
Dionysus may have lost their head, one side of consciousness, the side that retrieves things from the unconscious and brings them back. Woman retrieving the
golden dress must weave her Athena/Apollo side.
Psyche's third task was to retrieve golden fleece from
the rams. She knew not to do it in the height of the sun
but to wait until that time between day and night and
gather the golden wool from the thicket. The danger in
retrieving the aggression of the rams and total rational
consciousness of the Apollonian sun is that the other
side of the container will be overpowered. The golden
dress inter-laced with green ivy makes a place for both
sides.

The golden mask with the emerald green eyes of
W.B. Yeats led through unmasking the green peas to
the black pearl behind. But the treasure has still to be
brought back. Knowing that I first sighted it under clear
water at the base of a tree recalls that in the dream of
Sophia and the Clown the gigantic oak's roots were not
visible. She was angry, killing the clown side.

Something more is hidden, imprisoned at the root
of the oak tree, a spirit long bottled up about to pop the
cork and circulate in the veins of the bark.

The question is how to distill the spirit, turn the
water to wine. I recall the next move in the dream pattern—an incident I did not understand until now. I am
freeing a man from confinement. I arrange to let him
walk out straight down the main corridor without being
seen. On the way out we stop for lunch, a cup of oyster

sauce (the way soup comes together at the bar of the unconscious).

Behind the mask of the wizard, the magician, and the hero god, woman must learn in which direction to see.

Dorothy in search of a brain for her friend, the straw man, is given a doctorate in thinkology. In search of wisdom, behind the clown mask, I received a doctorate in foolishness, mirth, a-muse.

From Transference
to Transformation

"To move by way of transformation of consciousness is to build bridges between."

10

From Transference
to Transformation

Once one has peeled back the mask or looked through the eyes into the pure circle of blackness running through the eyes of all masks one may turn and look through the masks from the other side seeing with the eyes through which the God sees. The reverse side of this movement is the Freudian projection and retrieval of one's potentialities for selfhood from the mask of the God. It is the latter that has all too often directed the course of twentieth century theology, creating a subject-object dualism between self and God. Rather the move should be to no longer seek to see the God endowed with or stripped of the self's highest potentialities, sex, or color but to seek to see as the God sees.

Metaphor is a transference of a name from one thing to another, a movement across. Metaphor is a bridge between naming self and naming God. Yet we must journey, as Joseph Campbell says, into "the unknown beyond both the image of God and the image of self in order to discover the ultimate ground of all these guiding and protecting, edifying, yet imprisoning names and forms."[1]

Both the spirit of God and the spirit of self have become imprisoned in the traditional names and forms and the spell needs to be broken. The metaphoric bridge between is all that is left when the old banks have lost their name and place.

In light of the theme of the grail quest weaving in and out of my dreams, I recall that the spirit of the King is weakened or he is dying, while at the same time his magician, Merlin, allows himself to be imprisoned in an oak tree, enchanted by his dark anima Vivien (who from another perspective is the holy Lady of the Lake). To be spell-bound is to let one's potentiality for being in the world be trapped by one's fascination with another person, place, or thing. Hence spell-binding is the older parallel to our contemporary transference phenomena.

The flip side of transference is transformation. The spirit of being manifest through persons, places, or things is revelation for those who can see. Paul Tillich wrote: "Revelation is not information about divine things; it is the ecstatic manifesting of the Ground of Being in events, persons, and things. Such manifestations have shaking, transforming, and healing powers."[2]

The task at hand is the transformation of human consciousness so as to ready the vessel for the God who needs a space to come to appearance. We are that vessel when the water flows.

The task of the alchemist was to free the world-creating spirit of God from physical nature. Our task is the reverse, to house the God in persons, places, and things without entrapment, allowing the move between underworld and earth, earth and sky. To move by way of transformation of consciousness is to build bridges between.

Once the Freudian movement backward to unmask our projections onto the God has been accomplished and the potentiality of selfhood retrieved, then the task is not, as Freud thought, to kill the Father God, but rather to let the God story within each of us begin to write the way forward.

What is new in emerging consciousness is the discovery that woman's heretofore imprisoned animus may contain the way to the image of the dark, hidden God.

In the first stage of woman's development there is no place for woman's animus, it is controlled by or contained in the image of the Great Mother. This is the stage where the giant woman casts out her animus hero, the double-faced clown: Christ/Hermes.

In the second stage of development there is a fixation on the father God, a transference of the woman's animus onto a paternal supreme being and thus a passive identification with the projected animus. Erich Neumann notes that even the spiritual father may take the mask of magician, holding woman captive, separating her from the world of reality, her home, and her own backyard. Here woman incurs the wrath of the Great Mother.[3] The Dionysian magician or wizard, containing her own animus, fascinates her and carries her away from her contact with the earth. Dorothy was intrigued by the Wizard and the possibility of a balloon trip before deciding to return home.

The problem in the second stage is lack of ego development. The ego must free itself in order to bring the animus into conscious relationship. Total identification of ego with animus is loss of soul into the unconscious, the abduction into underworld.

In the third stage of development, woman's animus simply shifts the projection from the father God to the son God or, in everyday life, from a father to a husband or son who is to live out her unlived potentialities. When projected onto another, the animus hides and makes impossible ego development. Dorothy's quest involves the development of her animus through her male friends: the straw man's quest for a brain, the tin man's quest for a heart, and the lion's quest for courage. Her quest ends with a confrontation, an unmasking, of the wizard who was to grant all these traits of selfhood.

The fourth stage is one of confrontation with the one who contains woman's animus potential. Psyche stops sleeping with a god in the dark and sheds a light, brings the dark side to consciousness. She then must perform the tasks of the hero herself, freeing her animus from her husband and her husband from his mother. The confrontation is not only with the dark god but also with the Great Mother.

The confrontation presupposes ego development, differentiation of consciousness, but also allows seeing the space of identity between self and god, leading to the quest for reunion.

Ego development involves getting in touch with the function of one's body, making a space for gathering those contents of the unconscious into reality. Here woman comes to understand her self as the creative matrix of all culture. If woman has indeed made a room for her animus potentialities, she contains within herself the creative space of all coming into being. What is released at the highest level of feminine consciousness is the woman's creativity, the birth space of new life.

Through identification with the mother goddess she finds the vessel, the grail, of all creative being; through the projection of self potential onto the father God she sees at a distance her infinite capabilities of being in the world; through the projection of her animus, onto the hero son god, or wizards, or magicians, or wise men, she first views her highest potential as culture creating hero; and finally through the developed ego which sees her self as the containment of all stages of existing, she may retrieve her lost soul projected outward. The treasure is learning to see the self and world anew now transformed by that retrieved energy of all creative being in the world.

This creative capacity of woman brought back to reality has the potential to heal the land through the concealed presencing of the god through persons, places, and things of the everyday earth. Things lighted now from the inside by a returned soul are transfigured.

Erich Neumann in "Creative Man and Transformation" defines "transfiguration" as "when things, a landscape or a work of art, come alive or 'grow transparent,' this signifies that they are transformed into what we have called 'unitary reality.' "[4]

The power of imaginal consciousness is a way of seeing anew the ordinary and the everyday as described by Wallace Stevens:

> Yet I am the necessary angel of earth since, in my sight, you see the earth again.[5]

Rainer Maria Rilke while polishing his piano has the creative vision:

> Under my zealous dust cloth, it suddenly started to purr mechanically . . . and its fine, deep black surface became more and more beautiful. When you've been through this there's little you don't know! . . . Politeness tinged with mischief was my reaction to the friendliness of these objects, which seemed happy to be so well treated, so meticulously renovated. And even today, I must confess that while everything about me grew brighter . . . I became newly aware, somehow, of the size of the room, reflecting it more and more clearly: pale gray and almost square . . . , well, yes, I felt moved, as though something were happening, something, to tell the truth, which was not purely superficial but immense, and which

touched my very soul: I was an emperor washing the feet of the poor, or Saint Bonaventure, washing dishes in his convent.[6]

Notes

1. Cited by Stanley Romaine Hopper, "Le cri de Merlin! or, Interpretation and the Metalogical," in *Anagogic Qualities of Literature*, ed. Joseph Strelka, *Yearbook of Comparative Literature*, Vol. IV (Pennsylvania: Pennsylvania State University Press, 1971).
2. Paul Tillich, "Reason and Revelation," Systematic Theology, Vol. I (Chicago: The University of Chicago Press, 1951).
3. Erich Neumann, "The Psychological Stages of Feminine Development," *Spring*, trans. Rebecca Jackson, rev. Hildegard Nagel and Jane Pratt (New York: The Analytical Psychology Club, 1959), p. 74.
4. Erich Neumann, "Creative Man and Transformation," *Art and the Creative Unconscious*, trans. Ralph Manheim, Bollingen Series LXI (Princeton: Princeton University Press, 1959), p. 175.
5. Wallace Stevens, "Angel Surrounded by Paysans," *The Collected Poems of Wallace Stevens* (New York: Alfred Knopf, 1965), p. 496.
6. Rainer Maria Rilke, "Lettres à une musicienne," quoted by Gaston Bachelard, *The Poetics of Space*, trans. Maria Jolas (Boston: Beacon Press), p. 70.

Between the Spheres

"The dream symbols have a double-meaning as a picture of the right and left hemisphere of the brain bridged by the corpus collosum passing through the center of the faculties. The image fits exactly diagrams from the back of the brain."

11

Between the Spheres

In my dream series I am still in quest of the pearl, that round philosopher's stone. A pivotal dream in the quest series takes place in the middle of the ocean between two spheres. The spheres parallel each other and are connected by double underwater paths in a tunnel and a double lane overwater bridge. As the dream opens I find myself in a well-lighted empty chapel on the right sphere. The chapel is shaped like a Christmas tree or the tip of a lance, another grail symbol. Suddenly as the light streams through the window I realize there is a thunderstorm and that I need to get to the other side before lightning strikes. As I ran across the top bridge with my golden retriever, the lightning struck the bridge just behind our heels. While running I noted a semi-circular gate house between the spheres in the center of the ocean with a shadow figure at the controls. Immediately after passing through the center I found myself on the underwater tunnel double tracks moving toward the left sphere, vaguely realizing there was food on the left side. The double tracks continued as I entered the cave on the left. It was a faculty center, dining place at a university. At the center of the faculty center there were tables on the left and a semi-circular alcove on the right. In the center of the base of the alcove hung a spiralled conch sea shell seen from the back side with the mother of pearl glistening. Behind the alcove, the stair well spiralled upward to another level. Although I knew the place of the pearl I could not yet retrieve it; I had to first follow the double tracks through the cave alongside my double self but never seeing it.

I later happened to read that one of the puzzling things Leonardo Da Vinci invented was a double spiral staircase which two people could ascend and descend without seeing each other.

Consciousness doubles at the threshold of creativity. Rather than regression, the return to the cave can be read as doubling. One returns to one's past to retrieve those elements which allow the creative move forward. The double self allows oneself to see itself reflected in another. Here one can retrive one's animus. Through creativity, that is the embodiment of one's hidden potential in some form, the woman's double manifests itself both as other and as her own, yet now not split off.

The doubleness of human consciousness often manifests itself in dream imagery as the simultaneous emergence of the double face of the god. In my own dream the god of death is juxtaposed with the source of life.

The dream opened in an empty chapel with the impending threat of lightning, the light of the god. At the time of the dream I had not read about the perilous chapel scene in the grail quest. Jessie Weston, in her work on the grail entitled *From Ritual to Romance*, notes that there is always some threat in the chapel. For Gawain it was a thunderstorm. She also notes that the chapel marks a crossway, sometimes located in a forest and sometimes located on an island in the middle of a body of water.[1] Clearly the location in forest or water points to a space of encounter within the depths of the unconscious, the space of danger as well as encounter with the god and self.

Another similarity between the dream and the grail story is Gawain's asking the meaning of the lighted tree in the perilous chapel. In my dream the whole chapel was in the shape of a Christmas tree or lance tip and was totally lighted by the distant lightning. Jung notes that most people fail to ask what the Christmas tree means: It is "mixed with the secret of the evergreen tree that carries the new-born Light . . . a serious answer would require a far-reaching dissertation about the antique symbolism of the dying god, and its relation to the cult of the Great Mother and her symbol, the tree . . . ."[2]

Weston interprets the chapel as the place of initiation between the self and God.[3] But the danger is in remaining too long there. The self cannot bear too much encounter. The lightning does kill.

Yet the lightning also points to new creation. It strikes through the bridge, fire hitting water, pointing to fertilization and new creation, Zeus' thunderbolt bringing life out of water. The spiral of the lightning is paralleled on the other side by the spiral of the sea shell and the stair, all symbols of sexual creation.

The sea shell is the containing vessel. From the back side, mother of pearl spiralled toward the center. I have found Mircea Eliade's work on the symbolism of shells most helpful in understanding the dream. Sea shells and the pearl, he notes, participate "in the sacred powers which are concentrated in the Waters . . . and in Woman."[4] The pearl obviously is the emerging child of the psyche and, according to Eliade, a symbol of a transcendent reality.[5] In ancient China the symbol of the deep water producing a pearl insures that the land will not wither.[6] I find this a most fitting combination in light of the quest for the grail being connected with healing the land. The shell basically symbolizes creative power, functioning as the universal matrix of all birth and rebirth.[7] A hymn of the *Atharva Veda* brings all the images of the dream together: ''Born of the wind, of the air, of the lightning, of the light, may the shell born from gold, the pearl, defend us from fear . . . . Jewel born of the sea . . . may it shield us on all sides from the arrows of the gods . . . .''[8] ''A tradition of Eastern origin explains the birth of the pearl as the child of lightning penetrating into a vessel, the pearl thus being the result of union between Fire and Water.''[9] The Goddess is born out of the sea shell. Christian symbolism speaks of the pearl as Christ the King and as the human soul[10] and as the symbol of the kingdom at hand.

Normally I have not mentioned what occasioned my dream imagery, but in this case the parallel between day thought and night thought may be useful for understanding. I had been teaching and studying intently the nature of creativity in relation to the movement between brain hemispheres. The dream symbols have a double-meaning as a picture of the right and left hemisphere of the brain bridged by the corpus collosum, passing through the center of the faculties. The image fits exactly diagrams from the back side of the brain. I was seeking specifically the function of a tiny pearl-like structure in the center of the thalamus (Greek for woman's room). I discovered that it was called the massa intermedia and its functions were unknown. However, it does serve as an inner passageway between thalami, perhaps a passage for our most archaic feelings, an inner bridge. This subject belongs to another book I am contemplating on *Woman's Brain*, but the coming together of the two books through dream image and brain structure triggered the move between hemispheres, perhaps the double space of creativity.

Notes

1. Jessie L. Weston, From *Ritual to Romance* (New York: Peter Smith, 1941), p. 165.
2. C.G. Jung, *Man and His Symbols* (New York: Dell Publishing Co., 1964), p. 69.
3. Weston, p. 172.
4. Mircea Eliade, *Images and Symbols* (New York: Sheed and Ward, 1969), p. 125.
5. Eliade, p. 126.
6. Eliade, p. 128.
7. Eliade, p. 131.
8. Eliade, p. 130.
9. Eliade, p. 148.
10. Eliade, p. 148.

Fouring Consciousness

"To quest for the grail is to quest for one's soul where the God presences. But one loses one's soul often during the quest by seeking its reflection in another, the problem of seeing one's double. To retrieve the other side of one's self requires double reduplication, the fouring of consciousness."

12

Fouring Consciousness

In ending I need to retrace where I began and to see if what has come between forms a bridge for new passage.

The bank on which much of contemporary theology rests is Freud's view that the father God is a transference of the self's need for protection and dependency. The assumption of Freud's psychoanalysis is that as one outgrows the need, one outgrows the God. Then theology either claims the death of the father God or speaks abstractly with Tillich of the God beyond the God of theism. All we know of this God is that the encounter presupposes the development of courage within the depths of one's self. Liberation theology may substitute black father for white father or mother goddess for father God, but the need of the self to outgrow the dependency on the transferred parent image remains the same.

Other stages of self-consciousness correlate with other images of the God. Thus far I have been attempting to see the correlation between the stages of transformation of woman's consciousness and the encounter with the God/gods/goddesses, supplementing

Freud's backward reduction with Jung's movement forward through the multiple images of God appearing through the depths of the unconscious. Specifically, I have been following the development of woman's consciousness through the processes of identification and differentiation set forth by Jung's disciple, Eric Neumann.

It is Neumann's second stage of feminine development, the stage of woman's being overpowered by the encounter with the masculine other that correlates with Freud's view of a fixed stage of encounter with the masculine father God. According to Neumann, the woman may fixate at this second stage, seeing herself forever as the daughter of a protecting or threatening father. But in the natural course of development she should move beyond this infantile relation. Freud for some reason assumes this is the only relation possible to the father god and thus he must be killed to make room for the ascension of the son. Because the Oedipal paradigm of the God being correlated with self-development by Freud does not hold for feminine development, it is necessary to look elsewhere for the myth structure for women.

Woman moves beyond the stage of dependency on a protecting father figure by transferring her potential onto an external hero, usually male (but times are changing!). Here she sees her unlived self embodied in the other and often falls in love with the reflection. Or the embodiment of her potentials in someone else may silence all those potentials in herself, leaving her speechless and in awe of her hero. Here Dionysus is noted for his embodiment of the nature of woman as well as man. Woman who has not developed her own ego may follow this Pied Piper into madness; for a woman who has developed the other side of herself the encounter may lead to the birth of creativity. In Christian theology the move is usually from worship of a father God to worship of a son God. This may be simply an extension of the transference and thus lead to worship of an idol and the cessation of self-development. The other side of the picture is that the Son may indeed embody the highest creative possibility of women's soul; here she is like Christ, her potential to mediate God's presence.

In the fourth stage of consciousness, woman must move to actualization of the other side of herself, her animus or soul. Even the Jungians have been remiss in not developing the positive manifestation of woman's animus. If what woman has been projecting onto a father and a son God is a reflection of the potentiality of her own deepest self, then a phenomenology of the images of woman's emerging animus should open new images of the God who is underground in our time. Such images are beginning to appear in the dreams and creativity of women, surfacing from the depths of the unconscious.

The task is to retrieve one's own soul and, in so doing, create the space through which the God appears from the deep. The first step in catching one's soul is to recognize one's double. I do not understand this process totally, but I do see that what is in the unconscious is a double reversal of what is brought to consciousness. It may appear so opposite as not to belong to us at all, yet it is oneself seen from the other side. One has to learn to do a double take and a turn about as one retrieves the images. Perhaps one brain hemisphere mirrors the other and turns things around. Whatever the mechanism, it is the discovery Kierkegaard made when he spoke of looking into a mirror expecting to see an apostle looking back but an ape peered out instead.

It was only near the end of my dream quest that people actually reversed positions from that of their day life or that objects such as houses and pools appeared paired with their doubles. The first appearance was the double image of the Goddess Sophia, as wisdom and as fool, casting out her double shadow or animus, the clown/Christ. When the shadow is cast out it takes on a life of its own at the center of things.[1]

The double appears next as the brother of the Buddha, proclaiming knowledge as ignorance, reminiscent of Socrates' daimon. With the encounter everything began to double, even the direction of language. As he rolled forward the words read: "Knowledge is knowing what you do not know." Then he rolled backward and the sentence could be read backward. Meanwhile, I saw my dream self standing in the shadows saying: "He does not know what he is talking about." The conundrum threw me back on my self as I awakened laughing, the first step toward retrieving the clown side and the Buddha nature as two sides of the same.

The double movement appeared next as the car and the horse on two sides of the gas tank, and I realized that I was trying to fill the spirit with the wrong kind of horse power. I juxtaposed Kierkegaard's understanding of spirit as being like a spirited horse and Plato's parable of the self as the two horses of spirit and instinct yoked together but pulling in two directions guided by the charioteer of reason. I realized that the two would be split forever with reason as the guide, but doubling was possible if imagination took the reins. My golden retriever and my St. Bernard, joining the dispirited horse, healed the split, under the guide of imagination.

The doubling appears next as doubling back, retracing a path I had been before but now with a different vision. This was the return to Trafalgar Square, the place where the road circles the square. Circling the square is the process of bringing the unconscious to consciousness. In the square I encountered the masks onto which woman projects her animus. The mask was the golden and green dress on a manikin, the headless woman or the dwarf, which is the German meaning of the word. Walter Otto notes that Dionysus always appeared in the mask as "pure confrontation—an antipode, and nothing else. It has no reverse side—'Spirits have no back,' the people say." "Here there is nothing but encounter, from which there is no withdrawal—an immovable, spell-binding antipode."[2] The only way past the spell-binding is to go through the encounter, look through those eyes to the pure emptiness behind what is. If one can stand it one may stay on the dark track long enough to come to a turning, enabling one to see back through the eyes of the mask looking, as Rilke says, in the same direction as the god. This is the way to the other side and to the retrieval of one's soul or animus. The dress was woven of the Apollonian gold of consciousness and twined with the green Dionysian ivy from the underworld.

Unmasking Dionysus, or Dorothy's unmasking the wizard, is not unlike Psyche's shedding a light on the dark god. But there is a difference. Unmasking Dionysus and the wizard is like peeling an onion; one hits the pure nothing at the center of things. Psyche's movement is the reverse. She thought she was married to a beast and she encountered the god of love. Both movements are necessary.

Dorothy has to find her way back to reality and avoid staying in fantasy land forever through an inflation, a balloon trip. Ariadne, united with Dionysus at the center, knows the way through the underworld but must bring the product of their union back to reality. This creative birth is impossible without Apollonian consciousness.

Psyche, like Ariadne, is abandoned by the male god, and thus must become her own hero. Her task to bring back a vessel of water from the underworld triggered in my own psyche the parallel quest for the grail vessel and the need for water in the land.

Strangely enough, women were forbidden not only to quest for the grail but even to ask about it. Jessie Weston finds this unbelievable and tries to explain it by contamination of the legend with surrounding religions which excluded women. She says: "It does not appear to be in harmony with the prominent position assigned to women in the Grail ritual, the introduction of a female Grail messenger, or the fact that (with the exception of Merlin in the Barron text) it is invariably a maiden who directs the hero on his road to the Grail castle, or reproaches him for his failure there."[3] Ms. Weston's argument actually only confirms that women were usually used to inspire or guide the male hero rather than become the hero themselves. I am reminded of Jungians who only reach the stage of the purpose of woman's animus being to inspire man's quest for his own soul or anima.

The interesting note in Ms. Weston's remarks is that Merlin might serve as a guide for women on the quest. Merlin, the magician in the court of King Arthur, was enamored by a woman, Vivien, who tricked him into giving her the secret of his magic. She then turned his art on him and imprisoned this magi of the spirit in the oak tree where he remained. Today one thinks of four-fold transference and counter transference between male/female and anima/animus. The magician's art is spell-binding and Merlin failed to teach Vivien how to break the spell. Vivien seen from the other side is the Lady of the Lake, the woman who rears the hero of the grail, Lancelot. The story does not take us further, where the Lady of the Lake would herself become the hero rather than transferring that task onto her adopted son hero. Women simply have to use their imagination and leave the other side of themselves free at least to dream.

To quest for the grail is to quest for one's soul where the God is presence. But one loses one's soul often during the quest by seeking its reflection in another, the problem of seeing one's double. To retrieve the other side of one's self requires double reduplication, the fouring of consciousness.

This conscious return to one's double origins appeared in the dream of the double tracks moving through the cave of the faculty center. Not only did I have to move simultaneously on parallel tracks with my double and do the same thing, but in the movement we could not see each other. The double reduplication came from the other self, or side of the brain, which watched and understood the movement as it happened. In the first stage of unitary consciousness there is mother and child but the two appear as one. In the fourth stage of consciousness there is both differentiation and unity simultaneously, both hemispheres moving together. Beyond Jung and Neumann, I have found that not only does woman identify with the mother and the goddesses and differentiate herself as other from the male father or hero, but she also, in this fouring of consciousness, identifies through her soul, the animus other side, with the Father and the Son, or with any of the male gods such as Hermes, Dionysus, and Apollo. The final task is to retrieve the soul from the double identification, a second differentiation and the move beyond transference.

The dream that took me back to the place of origins of identification and the source of differentiation with the male gods was the image of being at the source of two rivers. At the source of the first river I watched Dionysus dance, but when I realized he was clothed in a mesh net I realized I could not dance and then found myself in a parallel river, yet it joined the Dionysian river at the source. There on the bottom of what was called Deep River was a square with four blocks, numbering the four beats to the rhythm so I could learn to dance. I needed this Apollonian structure to teach me the steps at this level of depth to help me avoid the entanglements with Dionysus leading the dance and my not knowing the way. Then in the dream I turned to what I thought was a third river and began to follow it, but it turned out to be all the tiny streams of water flowing down the side of a mountain that give rise to the two rivers. Above the streams mountain people were washing their clothes.

To lose oneself in the dance with the gods is not the way. The task is to find oneself in order to be able to follow the steps.

If there is only identity, the transferred soul, woman loses her head, the Dionysian maenad. The most difficult task is to differentiate oneself following double identification, with mother, father, or hero gods. This is to refuse inflation and return to everyday life. In the dream the mountain people were simply doing everyday chores, washing clothes, but one learns to see the steep path of the cleansing of the soul. The dream was my return to the Dionysian encounter, a repetition, a doubling, but with a new vision.

The movement I am talking about requires doubling, what Socrates called recollection and what Kierkegaard and Freud called repetition. In the moves backward Freud called the repetition regression. There is a possibility of a second return with consciousness transformed. Perhaps this is near Kierkegaard's second immediacy. Paul Ricoeur hinted at this fourfold movement, inspired by his dialectical reading of Hegel's phenomenology of consciousness and Freud's backward movement of regression. He inspired my interpretation by suggesting rereading Freud from the perspective of the "reduplication of consciousness."[4]

Ricoeur begins the process with a reference to Hegel's dialectic of "consciousness entering the process of self-recognition in another" and thus "it is doubled and becomes a self."[5] It is this self-recognition in the other that moves beyond Freud's view of projection or illusion. And it is a move beyond a reductionist view of transference.

Ricoeur helps me understand the scope of my quest by saying: "An exegesis of consciousness would consist in a progression through all the spheres of meaning that a given consciousness must encounter and appropriate in order to reflect itself as a self, a human, adult, conscious, self."[6] The self in seeking itself finds itself only in self-recognition through the other, be it God, Goddess, or another person reflecting its hidden self. Ricoeur cites Hegel's saying that self-consciousness is the " 'infinite realizing itself in and through consciousness' . . . . Each consciousness seeks itself in the other and 'does what it does only so far as the other does the same.' "[7] The latter sentence is an exact description of the dream process of the double self on double tracks doing only what the other did. The reduplication is when the conscious self, seeking to understand itself, recalls the double self from the unconscious self by way of the dream-symbol, a fourfold consciousness.

When a doubling appears in dreams and the doubles appear as two different figures, Jung says "the conscious ego-personality does not contain all the contents and components that it could contain."[8] Likewise the God image may not contain everything it ought to contain and thus may produce the split off double. Whereas Christ is the fish "drawn from the deep" there is also Leviathan, a fish-like monster dwelling in the depths.[9] A double movement is needed. Not only does the self learn to recognize its double, but simultaneously the self clears a space for incarnating the other side of the God.

Postscript

The dream cycle ended with two fishy images. In the first scene I am standing in the shadows watching a woman try to carpet the whole earth with transparent layers of a blue and green substance. She has put all the pieces back together except one, leaving a hole the size of a giant fish. In the shadows I stand with a small fish-shaped coaster in my back pocket ready to contribute, but it is large enough only to place one glass of water on.

In scene two I am sitting on the beach coast and an old man is about to teach me to fish. My line is behind me lying on the sand with the hook turned upward into the air. The waves come in and bring fish to rest on top of the hook. Three stacked themselves together on the one hook without my ever touching the line.

I looked at the definition of fishing in my *Dictionary of Symbols:* "Fishing amounts to extracting the unconscious elements from deep-lying sources—the 'elusive treasure' of legend, or, in other words, wisdom."[10]

Notes

1. Walter F. Otto, *Dionysus Myth and Cult* (Bloomington and London: Indiana University Press, 1965), p. 91.
2. Otto, p. 90.
3. Jessie L. Weston, *From Ritual to Romance* (New York: Peter Smith, 1941), p. 159.
4. Paul Ricoeur, *Freud and Philosophy: An Essay on Interpretation*, trans. Denis Savage (New Haven and London: Yale University Press, 1970), p. 483.
5. Ricoeur, p. 463.
6. Ricoeur, p. 463.
7. Ricoeur, p. 467, quoted from Hegel, *The Phenomenology of Mind*, trans. J. Baillie (rev. 2d ed. London, 1931), p. 230.
8. C.G. Jung, *Aion: Researches into the Phenomenology of the Self*, trans. R.F.C. Hull, 2d ed.; Bollinger Series XX (Princeton, N.J.: Princeton University Press), p. 185.
9. Jung, p. 185.
10. J.E. Cirlot, *A Dictionary of Symbols*, trans. Jack Sage, 2d ed.; (New York: Philosophical Library, 1962), p. 108.